Making Mus[ic with your]

APPLE MAC

Keith Gemmell

PC Publishing

PC Publishing
Keeper's House
Merton
Thetford
Norfolk IP25 6QH
UK

Tel 01953 889900
Fax 01953 889901
email info@pc-publishing.com
web site http://www.pc-publishing.com

First published 2005

© Keith Gemmell

ISBN 1 870775 95 3

British Library Cataloguing in Publication Data
A catalogue record for this book is available from the British Library

Cover design by Hilary Norman Design Ltd

Printed and bound in Great Britain by Biddles, Kings Lynn, Norfolk

Contents

Introduction

All new Macs are suitable for music making. You can walk into your nearest Apple dealer, or visit the Apple website and order one of six brand new machines confident in the knowledge that when you get it home you can use it as a digital audio workstation, almost straight out of the box.

You don't necessarily need any extra hardware to begin making music on a new Mac because, apart from the iBook, the entire range comes complete with 'audio line in' and headphone sockets. Just plug in a guitar or microphone and you can start recording and mixing your songs immediately, using GarageBand, a virtual recording studio which ships free across the entire Apple Mac range, as part of the iLife suite. After mixing your tunes you can burn them to CD, using iTunes. Yes, you really can do all this on a single computer.

But which Mac do you choose? Can you record songs on a humble eMac or do you need a top-of-the-range G5 machine? Which Mac? (chapter 1) has the answers, demystifies the technical jargon, and in conjunction with the Music Maker's Spec Sheets (Appendix), will help you select the right machine for your particular musical purposes. Each computer in the Mac range is examined and evaluated purely from the perspective of music making.

Do you need an audio interface or can you get by using the Mac's built-in audio connections? Choosing and configuring the right hardware peripherals to actually get audio into and out of your Mac can be a bewildering experience. A singer/song-writer, working alone, doesn't necessarily need the same facilities as a band member recording a live gig. Setting up your Studio (chapter 2) delves into the world of USB and FireWire interfaces, keyboard controllers, preamps, mics, speakers and headphones. There's also a short tutorial on configuring your studio with Apple's AMS (Audio MIDI Setup).

Every new Mac ships with GarageBand, an easy-to-use recording package packed with hundreds of instruments and loops. If you've never used a sequencer to record music before, Making Music with GarageBand (chapter 3) will put you on the right track. Building arrangements, recording guitars and vocals, using Apple Loops and GarageBand software instruments, adding effects and mixing – all these subjects are discussed in detail. In fact Making Music with GarageBand is rather like a book within a book.

GarageBand 2 is now with us and boasts a bevy of new features including pitch adjustment and time-stretching tools. GarageBand 2 – what's new? (chapter 4) provides the low-down.

As brilliant as GarageBand is, any music software that's given away with a new computer is bound to have some limitations. You'll need to look further afield for full control of your external MIDI gear, audio editing, working with video and virtual mixing controls. In Beyond GarageBand (chapter 5) we take a look at the three major sequencing packages for the Mac – Logic, Cubase and Digital Performer.

Should you buy a professional score package such as Sibelius or will something simple like Finale NotePad suffice? Can you produce convincing scores using just your sequencing software? What about publishing your scores on the Internet – can it be done? All is revealed in Score Writing and Self-publishing (chapter 6).

One of the best things about making music on the Mac is the immediate contact with the outside world. Write and record a song in GarageBand, save it to iTunes and putting it on the Internet is just a few steps away. Getting Your Music Out There (chapter 7) shows you how to tag your files, making them Internet-ready, encode them as MP3s, burn them to CD and make them available to millions, on the Web.

Which Mac?
A look at the Apple Macintosh range of computers and their suitability for music

O kay, I know what you're thinking. With all those smart new Macs to choose from, all capable of capturing pristine quality audio, how do you know which one is right for you? It's a good question. After all you don't want to spend any more money than you have to. Buying a top of the range G5 is not necessarily the best move if you only intend to use it for recording a few songs in GarageBand. On the other hand, neither do you want to spend your hard earned money on a new eMac only to find that it doesn't quite do everything you hoped it might. So, before you decide on a particular model, let's take a look at some of the things you need to look for on the spec sheets.

Brain power

All Apple Apple Macs have a powerful processor. Some Power Macs have two. Think of the processor as the brain of a computer, the part that does all the hard work, handling the data and directing signals between the different components of the machine. Audio recording software, including GarageBand, typically requires lots of this processing power. Take a look at the Music Maker's spec sheets (Appendix 1) and you'll see that all new Macs come with a powerful processor as standard. The Power Mac G5 machine even features dual processors. Nothing to worry about here then. You can buy any new Mac confident in the knowledge that it will run GarageBand and all but the most demanding high-end audio software with ease.

Memory matters

RAM (Random Access Memory) is the area of your computer where anything that needs processing is kept in temporary storage, ready for instant access by the CPU (Central Processing Unit). That includes the operating system, any open application programs and data currently in use, such as your audio files. If you shut down your computer or the system crashes, all the data held in the RAM area will be lost which is why we always frequently save our work – don't we?

Generally speaking, if you're working with audio you need as much RAM as you can get. 256MB of RAM is the absolute minimum requirement for running most audio software applications and many require 512MB. Although the entire Mac range ships with a minimum of 256MB, if you can afford to, order more when you purchase a new machine. You can of course always install additional memory at a later date. On the Power Mac machines it's a simple matter of opening up the case and fitting DIMMs (Dual Inline Memory Modules) into slots on the main logic board. On eMacs, iMacs and portables, easily accessed memory expansion slots are provided instead.

Hard drives

Multitrack digital audio recording requires a large drive. Audio files consume space at alarming rates and a complete stereo CD will probably occupy around 600 to 700 MB of hard disk space. Fortunately all new Macs come with enormous hard drives. 30GB is the minimum specification on the iBook and that's probably more than enough for most people.

But it's not just the size of the hard disk that's important. Speed is vital too, for transferring the data from the hard drive to your audio hardware. The key specification to look for here is the disk rotation speed which like the speed of old fashioned record players is measured as rpm (revolutions per minute). The faster the rotation speed of the disk the sooner the audio data is read. A speed of 5,400 rpm is considered reasonable for comfortably managing 16 tracks of audio in a sequencer such as Logic. This is variable of course and also depends to a large extent on the processor speed and the amount of RAM available on your computer. Disk speeds on the current Mac range vary between 4,200 rpm, on the iBook to 7,200 rpm on the Power Mac G5 machines.

CD/DVD drives

DVD drives are now standard on Apple Macs and as far as music making is concerned that's a good thing. Software developers like Yellow Tools, Ultimate Sound Bank and MOTU (Mach 5) are now supplying the sample sound content for their virtual instruments on DVD. That way they can supply better quality and larger libraries than if they just used CDs. This trend is certain to continue and sooner or later musicians without access to a DVD drive will be at an obvious disadvantage.

Apple provide you with a choice of either a Combo Drive or a SuperDrive when you purchase a new machine with the exception of the Power Mac G5 which comes with a SuperDrive as standard. Both drives will burn and read CD-R and CD-RW disk types. The Combo Drive also reads DVDs but if you need to burn one, either for storing audio files or digital images you'll need to buy a machine equipped with a SuperDrive. You can of course purchase a third party DVD-R drive from manufacturers such as Lacie but check the specifications first because they don't always work with iDVD, Apple's entry level DVD authoring software.

The big picture

In recent years music software packages available for the Mac such as Cubase SX/SL and Logic have become increasingly more powerful with dozens of features added with each new version. Apart from the obvious demands on your computer's CPU all the extra goodies such as virtual instruments, mixers and effects racks take up more and more of your computer monitor's precious screen space.

Of course you can always get round the problem to a certain extent by altering the screen resolution of your monitor to 1280 x 1024 (System Preferences > Display). However it's not ideal. Software plug-ins and virtual instruments are often crammed with features and reading the text is sometimes difficult enough at 1056 x 792 let alone anything smaller. So, monitor size and screen space should be a consideration when you're choosing a new Mac.

Generally speaking the larger the screen, the better working with audio applications is going to be. However, if you're musical ambitions are modest and you're happy just working with GarageBand you'll not experience the problem. In GarageBand most of the action takes place in a single user interface. There's no separate mixer, to make space for, just simple volume and pan controls associated with each track. Neither do the virtual instruments and effects units have fancy interfaces with hundreds of knobs and switches. Instead, Apple have adopted a list and menu based approach with simple sliders and value displays. Quite refreshing really.

Figure 1.1
Logic's arrange page, mixer and plug-ins are easier to work with using a 1280 x 1024 screen resolution

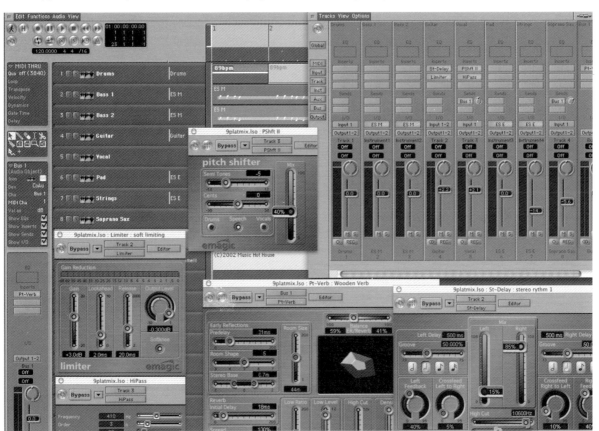

Getting audio in and out

Yes it's true. Just as it says on Apple's website, you really can record audio directly into your computer using GarageBand. Because all new Macs, apart from the iBook, have a line in jack, recording your voice or an acoustic instrument is a simple matter of connecting a microphone and recording an audio track. You can connect electric instruments too, such as keyboards, sound modules and synthesisers. You can even buy a special cable to connect your guitar directly to the audio in jack.

It's worth noting however that when recording directly, using the audio line in on G4 machines (eMacs, iBooks and PowerBooks), you're limited to 16-bit stereo and a 44.1-kHz sampling rate. Now that's CD quality, and as such it's fine for many recording projects. It's also the audio resolution supported by GarageBand. However professional recording software such as Logic offers an audio resolution up to 24 bit/192-kHz resolution and to take advantage of it you'll need an external audio interface of some kind.

Obviously, you need to monitor your performance when recording and listening to the playback. Now, although you can use the built-in speakers provided on most Macs, if you're serious about getting an accurate, well balanced mix of your songs use the headphone socket instead. But you don't necessarily have to use it for headphones alone. This stereo out jack can also be used to send the audio signal to an external mixer or speaker system.

A much better way to record audio and monitor the results is to use a USB or FireWire audio interface. You can connect mics, instruments and route audio to a speaker system using a device such as M-Audio's Omnistudio USB or Firewire Audiophile.

For more serious multitrack work PCI slots can be used to connect professional audio sound cards such as the M-Audio Delta 1010. But these can only be found on the G5 Power Macs. You'll also find a PC Card/CardBus slot on the portable PowerBooks (15 and 17-inch models) which can be used connect certain PCI audio interfaces.

Making connections

Your new Mac might be an all-in-one recording solution but it will not be long before you need to connect at least one peripheral device (almost a certainty if you own an iBook). Connectivity is an important factor when it comes to choosing a computer for music making. Fortunately all new Apple Macs come with a fair sprinkling of USB and FireWire connections. That said, on the average audio workstation, you can't have too many of them. Audio/MIDI interfaces, USB keyboards and software protection keys are just a few of the devices you're likely to accrue as your new digital audio workstation expands over time.

All new Macs have at least two USB 2.0 ports and if you purchase a model that features a separate keyboard, like the eMac, you'll find a couple of USB 1.1 connections on the keyboard itself. Two USB 2.0 ports can also be found on all three of Apple's new Cinema Display monitors. As far as music and audio are concerned the devices you're most likely to connect to USB ports are MIDI interfaces, synthesisers, MIDI controllers, audio/MIDI interfaces and software protection keys.

All new Apple Macs have at least one FireWire 400 port. Two FireWire ports can also be found on all three of Apple's new Cinema Display monitors. As far as music and audio are concerned, audio interfaces and mp3 players like the iPod are the devices you're most likely to connect to a FireWire port.

Info

USB is short for Universal Serial Bus a standard data transfer protocol which has been with us since 1996. Because it's a standard, third party hardware is supported on both Mac and PC platforms. Of course, different software is required for the various operating systems involved. USB 1 supports data transfer rates of 12 mbps (million bits per second) and will support up to 127 peripheral devices. USB 2 is a high speed version, introduced in 2001 and supports data transfer rates of up to 480 mbps. Apart from the speedy performance of USB 2 in general it also provides hot-plugging, which means that you can connect and disconnect USB devices without powering down your computer. And because it also provides power to the bus, you can power an audio/MIDI interface, like the M-Audio Audiophile USB, without using its AC power adaptor.

Info

FireWire is an extremely fast type of serial port developed by Apple and Texas Instruments. Also known as the IEEE 1394 standard it's capable of supporting chains of up to 63 devices. The original spec provided speeds up to 400 Mbps (million bits per second) but the new spec, known as 1394b, provides a blistering 3200 mbps. This makes it a good choice for high bandwidth applications including audio transfer.

Another advantage of this protocol is that it supports plug and play connections, hot swapping and the ability to provide power to connected peripheral devices. However, daisy chaining too many devices can lead to a degradation of the audio quality and is not generally recommended. FireWire is similar to USB in many ways but although it's much faster, it's more expensive.

Okay, armed with the above information, let's take a look at the individual computers available in the Mac range and assess their suitability for making music.

The eMac

Although the eMac's just an entry level computer let's not be snobbish about it. A quick look at our Music Maker's spec sheet for the eMac (see the Appendix) reveals a powerful processor (1.25 GHz PowerPC G4) and a reasonably fast hard drive with 40 GB of disk space. So, with specs like that you'll have no problems recording audio tracks and using GarageBand's Apple Loops and software instruments, providing you're sensible. In the case of the base model, which ships with just 256 MB of RAM, being sensible means keeping a check on the amount of audio tracks used in a project. If you write long songs or intend recording lots of instruments and loops you'll get better results if you order extra memory at the outset. Configurations of 512MB and 1GB are available so why not treat yourself and go for the 1GB option.

Figure 1.2
The eMac is a great entry level computer for desktop music making (pic courtesy of Apple).

Tip

To get an idea of how many audio tracks your computer can cope with before locking up and even crashing, load and play the various GarageBand demos.

Tip

If you're a music teacher, why not pay a visit to www.apple.com/education/garageband/lesson_plans? You'll find a range of lesson plans here created by teachers at elementary, middle and high school levels. Many of these are adaptable and make good starting points for teachers who prefer writing their own lesson material.

Even though eMacs have a 17-inch screen, you only get to view 16 inches. This is fine if you're using GarageBand, which has a clutter free interface. However programs like Cubase and Logic are easier to use with a larger screen. That said, it's no big deal if you're happy to 'make do' and don't mind occasionally dragging a few windows around the screen.

On the always important connectivity front, another glance at the Music Makers spec sheet tells us that the eMac has two FireWire ports and a total of five USB ports: three on the computer and two on the keyboard. No problem there then.

eMacs in school

The eMac was originally designed for the education sector, and now, with the inclusion of GarageBand, it's an excellent computer for music teachers and pupils at all levels.

Music teachers in the UK are sometimes tempted by the audio retail industry into spending vast sums of money on a few powerful desktop PCs for the classroom, along with high end software and racks of unnecessary recording equipment. It's arguable that a room full of inexpensive eMacs might serve them better. They're already very popular in US schools where educational site licenses are very competitively priced. That applies here in the UK too. However, music teachers often neglect to search for the deals, which admittedly, are not widely advertised and difficult to find on Apple's website. Should they persevere, they might be pleasantly surprised.

For the older, more advanced students, who have perhaps outgrown GarageBand, eMacs are still a viable option. They're perfectly capable of running Logic and Cubase, for audio/MIDI sequencing, and popular notation software such as Finale and Sibelius.

eMacs at home

Apart from their obvious attraction as educational tools, eMacs also make great home computers and entry level digital audio work stations, just so long as you don't make to many demands upon them. Amateur musicians, singer-songwriters and aspiring dance music producers will find them ideal for recording, either for pure pleasure or for making demos to promote their talents to a wider audience. That said, eMacs are also an excellent choice for professional musicians, as an all purpose computer. You see, not all musicians are interested in or require a state-of-the-art digital recording studio. They just need to get ideas down, make demos and print scores. And for those tasks, the eMac is ideal.

The iMac

The iMac started life as a rather odd looking (some would say ugly) computer but it's recently had a radical makeover. Now sporting sleeker looks and a G5 processor (1.6 GHz and 1.8 GHz) it's considerably more powerful than it's G4 predecessor. According to the Apple website, compared with the old iMac, the new G5 version plays 71% more simultaneous software instrument tracks in GarageBand. However, they don't mention its performance with simultaneous audio tracks. But

Figure 1.3
The iMac G5 17- and 20-inch models are capable of fulfilling most musician's home recording needs (pic courtesy of Apple).

with a G5 under the hood it shouldn't be a problem, unless you're pushing it to extremes.

The base model iMac ships with just 256MB of RAM. Now, if you're buying an iMac, as opposed to an eMac, you're probably a little bit more serious about recording. In that case you're likely to be recording larger projects in GarageBand, and you'll almost certainly need to buy extra RAM. Fortunately, that's not a problem because the iMac supports up to 2GB of RAM, which is enough to keep most musicians happy.

If you outgrow GarageBand – which is after all, an entry level recording package – programs like Cubase and Logic beckon. These programs are much easier to use with a larger screen. You're better off with an iMac than an eMac in this respect because on an iMac, a 17-inch screen means a full 17-inch viewing area (not 16 inches). That said, if you intend using music software, other than GarageBand, why not go for the luxury of the 20-inch version? You'll also get the extra grunt of the 1.8 GHz processor.

On the audio connection front, if you're thinking about buying an iMac, it's worth noting that the headphone jack doubles as an optical digital out which is handy for transferring your masters to a DAT machine.

Although popular with schools and colleges, the first G4 iMac never became a home studio favourite amongst musicians. However, the new G5 version will probably change that. It's a fast machine and has enough USB and FireWire ports to connect an audio interface, MIDI keyboard controller and software protection devices. In fact, if you're setting up a small project studio and your budget will not extend to a Power Mac, the new iMac is a perfectly respectable alternative. You'll not have quite as much raw power nor the flexibility of the larger computer but sensibly used, the iMac is capable of fulfilling most musician's home recording needs.

The iBook

Portable computers are enormously popular, for obvious reasons. The iBook is no exception and a favourite with young people. It looks cool, slips easily into a backpack, and if hooked up to a FireWire interface like the MOTU 828 makes for a super mobile recording studio. However, as far as audio recording is concerned the

Figure 1.4
The iBook G4 provides a portable working environment for musicians working away from home (pic courtesy of Apple).

average laptop will always be slightly inferior to it's desktop counterpart. In this respect, with the choice of a 1.2 GHz or 1.33 GHz G4 processor you could say the iBook falls somewhere between the eMac and iMac in terms of power. However, it lacks the peripheral connectivity of both those machines.

Like all the new Apple Macs the base model iBook ships with 256MB of RAM which these days isn't enough to run most music software. But, you can expand its memory capacity to 1.25 GB and buying as much memory as you can afford is always a wise move with portables used for audio.

Obviously a portable computer is not going to have the display area associated with most desktops. It's not a problem with GarageBand but if you're using an application such as Logic, arranging mixers and software instruments on a 14-inch screen can be tiresome. On a 12-inch display it's downright frustrating. That said, with location recording it's easier to live with because usually, only one window is open at a time in Logic or Cubase. The mixing is done later at home or in the studio, where the recorded work can be transferred to an iMac or Power Mac. Another solution is to hook up a second monitor to the iBook's VGA output. However, let's not nit-pick. Plenty of people make do with a 12-inch screen.

And the iBook audio connections? There aren't any. You have to use a USB or FireWire interface. That's fine because generally speaking it's a far easier, better quality solution for recording and monitoring anyway. However, the iBook is limited to just a single FireWire port and two USB 2.0 ports. Now, with the increasing trend among music software developers to use USB protection keys you may find yourself running out of ports to connect your audio and MIDI devices. The obvious way round this is to use a USB hub. But tests have proved that most USB hubs fail to support audio devices. Never mind, Griffin Technology, who specialise in audio USB solutions, manufacture the Griffin 4-Port which they say, solves the problem. You can find out more about it at http://www.griffintechnology.com.

Of all the Apple Macs the iBook is probably the least suitable machine for the home or project studio. It lacks the grunt of the iMac and the base model offers no more power than an eMac and fewer connection ports. But the purpose of laptops, of course, is to provide a portable working environment. And for musicians away from home who need a portable machine for writing and recording it's the perfect solution.

The PowerBook

Apart from their good looks and slim line dimensions Apple's three PowerBooks offer a good deal of power (G4 1.5GHz or 1.67Hz PowerPC G4) and a reasonable helping of RAM (512MB). However, these days, even 512MB is not enough memory for serious audio work. Fortunately the memory capacity is expandable on all three models with support for up to 2GB of RAM on the 15 and 17-inch models and 1.25GB on the 12-inch version.

Although capacious enough for full scale recording projects the 60GB and 80GB hard disks are not super fast at 5400 rpm. For really serious multitrack work, where many tracks have to be recorded in a single pass, you'll have more peace of mind and obtain better results by connecting a fast hard drive to the FireWire 800 port (see below).

Figure 1.5
The PowerBook G4 with 12- 15- and 17-inch displays are now established as a firm favourite with musicians and media professionals (pic courtesy of Apple).

There's plenty of screen space on the 17-inch model for Cubase, Logic and software samplers such as MOTU's MachFive although on the 15 inch, things are a little cramped. But it's worth noting that PowerBooks support dual display mode and you can extend your work area by connecting to an external display such as a TV or projector.

On the connectivity front, all models feature a FireWire 400 port, and two USB 2.0 ports. In addition, the 15-inch and 17-inch models include a FireWire 800 port. Using this to connect a fast external hard drive will significantly increase your PowerBook's audio performance.

The FireWire 800 protocol is faster than USB 2.0 (480Mbps) so if you can afford it, go for something like the Yamaha i88x as your PowerBook audio interface. This will leave the two USB ports free for MIDI devices and software protection keys. However, you might need to use a USB hub if more than one software protection key is occupying the USB ports.

As an alternative to a FireWire interface, using the PowerBook's PC Card slot, you can hook up an RME Multiface or Digiface audio card. RME have developed their own PCMCIA type II card as a go-between. Echo Digital offer a similar system with laptop adapters for their Layla audio cards.

The usual audio line in and headphone jacks are in evidence on the PowerBooks (both supporting 16-bit stereo and a 44.1-kHz sampling rate). But with the recent inclusion of digital in/out, for serious audio work, the 17-inch model is the one to go for. The built-in speakers are fine for general listening but obviously, not good enough for critical monitoring and mixing.

PowerBooks are now established as a firm favourite with musicians and media professionals the world over and function perfectly well as desktop replacements in the project studio. After all, many professional studios have been recording with PowerBooks and other portables for years that ran at half the speed of today's models.

PowerBooks are popular with musicians on the road too and are commonly used on-stage, running virtual audio and MIDI tracks. Professional keyboard players also use them, usually in conjunction with Logic, as a host for their virtual software instruments. They're a favourite too with sound engineers who use them as the heart of their mobile recording rigs. Of course, the PowerBook G4 is never quite going to match the Power Mac G5 and a there will always be a few trade-offs. But as long as you're aware of them and prepared to compromise occasionally, the PowerBook makes an excellent digital audio workstation.

The Power Mac G5

Okay we've reached the zenith of the Apple Mac range. The Power Mac G5 is used extensively by creative professionals throughout the world and can be found in publishing houses, photographic studios, science laboratories, film and video post production suites and of course recording studios. So if serious creative work is on the agenda, this is the machine to use.

The main considerations for audio recording and processing are well catered for on the Power Mac G5 spec sheet – a 64-bit processor with a very fast frontside bus, high-bandwidth architecture, and plenty of high-speed memory (as an aside, you may like to know that these machines will outperform even the fastest Pentium 4-based desktop computers). Until recently you could only buy dual processor models but you can now choose from a 1.8Ghz single processor as well as the more powerful dual processor 1.8GHz, 2GHz or 2.5GHz machines.

If you're opting for a Power Mac, then it's obvious that you intend doing some

Figure1.5
The Power Mac G5 is at the heart of top recording studios the world over (pic courtesy of Apple).

serious writing and recording. And that being the case, you'll also be running some pretty serious software such as Logic 7 or Cubase SX3. Both these programs require a minimum of 512MB of RAM and frankly, for a guaranteed trouble free performance you'll be better of ordering 1GB from the start, particularly if you opt for the 1.8GHz single processor machine which only comes with 256MB of RAM as standard.

The Power Mac's hard drives are fast (7200 rpm) and large enough for the most demanding audio work (80GB on the 1.8GHz and 160GB on the 2GHz and 2.5GHz) In fact, according to Apple the they support more audio tracks and plug-ins than any previous Power Mac.

As you'd expect on Apple's flagship computer, all Power Mac's come with a SuperDrive. However, they don't come with a monitor as standard. But you do have an excellent choice of 20, 23 and 30-inch flat screen Cinema Displays, all large enough for a screen full of sequencing software and audio plug-ins. If you intend doing sound-to-picture work you'll also find their DVI connections useful. Using these, you can connect two displays together.

Each Cinema Display also includes a FireWire 400 hub and a USB 2.0 hub, both with two ports. This considerably expands the number of peripheral devices you can add to your studio set-up.

Apart from its raw power another reason to choose the G5 for your studio is the generous amount of PCI expansion slots it offers. Unless you opt for a FireWire device this is where you will insert your sound card card and other audio peripherals. All models have a minimum of three open full-length 33MHz 64-bit slots. In addition, the 2GHz and 2.5GHz systems also have a 133MHz, 64-bit slot and two 100MHz, 64-bit slots.

FireWire is one of the fastest peripheral standards and because of its high bandwidth more and more pro audio companies are manufacturing FireWire interfaces. You'll have no problems connecting any of them to a Power Macs because they all have one FireWire 400 port on the front and one on the back of the case. In addition, there's a FireWire 800 port, also on the back. FireWire 800 throughputs data at a speed of 800 Mbps, twice that of FireWire 400. FireWire cables also carry power so you can use the Power Mac G5 to recharge your PowerBook's batteries, even while you're working.

Three USB 2.0 ports (one on the front and two on the back) and two USB 1.1 ports (on the keyboard) can be used to connect to audio interfaces, instruments, keyboards, microphones, speakers, and other audio peripherals.

Something you'll not find on many personal computers is the built-in optical S/PDIF I/O. This can be used to connect a variety of digital equipment including surround sound speaker systems and DAT machines. Transferring digital audio via an optical connection ensures pure, noise-free results because the data is transmitted as impulses of light, not electrical signals. A headphone mini jack on the front panel and high quality stereo analogue audio in and out ports on the rear complete the audio connections.

The Mac mini

The tiny Mac mini is just 16.5 cm wide and a little over 5 cm tall and must be about the smallest computer you can buy. It comes with either a 1.25GHz or 1.42GHz

Info

The Power Mac G5 supports more audio tracks and plug-ins than any previous Power Mac, in fact, three times that of it's predecessor, the G4. The dual 2.5GHz, dual 2GHz, dual 1.8GHz and single 1.8GHz Power Mac G5 systems can play 180, 159, 144 and 85 plug-ins, respectively, compared with a maximum of 60 plug-ins on the dual 1.42GHz Power Mac G4, the fastest Power Mac G4 Apple produced.

Info

If you happen to a have PC in your studio and it's graphics card supports DVI with DDC technology for wide screen viewing, it will probably be suitable for use with Apple's 20 and 23-inch Cinema Displays.

Figure 1.6
The Mac mini (pic courtesy of Apple).

PowerMac G4 processor. In fact, if you opt for the latter version, you'll have a potentially faster computer than either the eMac or the iBook. But what's really amazing is the price – just £339 ($499).

So what's the catch? Well, you have to buy the keyboard, mouse and monitor display separately. But the really neat thing is that if you already have a VGA monitor, you can plug it into the Mac mini's VGA adaptor. That means you can hook it up to almost any old CRT monitor or LCD flat panel display. You can also use it with a TV screen. This machine then is clearly intended to tempt Windows users with ageing PCs to switch to the Mac platform. But what about its music making potential?

The Mac mini may be small but it's just as capable of running GarageBand and Logic as the other G4 machines and comes with a capacious hard drive (40GB or 80GB). Its shortfall however is on the connectivity front although with one FireWire 400 and two USB 2.0 ports the average home studio user should be able to get by well enough. But with no audio line in facilities an audio/MIDI interface will, of course, occupy one of these ports. You'll have no problem getting audio out of the Mac mini though because it has a dual purpose headphone/audio line out. It also has a built-in speaker.

It's just a thought but the Mac mini could prove to be a handy interim machine for Cubase SX users considering the switch from Windows to Mac OS X because SX, like Finale and Sibelius, is a dual platform program.

Setting up your studio

O kay, you've taken delivery of a brand new Apple Mac computer and you can't wait to start recording with GarageBand. But where do you begin? Can you simply plug in a microphone or guitar and begin recording? At it's most basic level yes, as long as you're not too concerned about the quality of the audio.

The built-in audio connections – are they good enough?

GarageBand is an entry level sequencer and you can 'get by' with an entry level studio set-up using your Mac's limited built-in audio facilities. You see, because it only supports 16-bit recording, you can also 'get by' without the expense of a top-of-the-range audio interface. So just how do you get audio in and out of GarageBand 'on-the-cheap', so to speak?

Let's start with microphones. You've probably noticed that your new Mac has a built-in mic. Now, it's not up to much, quality-wise, but if you're a complete beginner to recording, it will get you started. Just don't expect sonic perfection because you'll not get it.

You can also connect a microphone directly to your computer's audio in jack but you'll almost certainly need an adaptor of some kind like the GarageBand Microphone Cable from Griffin Technology. That's because all Mac input jacks are 1/8-inch (3.5 mm). Although the results are probably going to be a big improvement over recording with the built-in mic, you should also be aware that the audio mini-jack's prime function is for hooking up consumer products such as CD players. In other words, you'll achieve acceptable but not remarkable results. The audio signal will almost certainly pick up noise from the electrical circuitry within the computer.

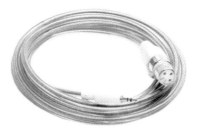

Figure 2.1
The GarageBand Microphone Cable can be used to plug a microphone into your Apple Mac's audio in mini-jack

And what about monitoring? Well, your new Mac does have built-in stereo speakers (unless you own a PowerMac which has just a front mounted mono speaker). But obviously, if you're recording your voice over a backing track you don't want the sound from the speakers being re-recorded onto your vocal track as well. To mute the speakers, plug in a decent set of headphones and monitor your performance that way. Also, although the built-in speakers are fine for general listening they're not good enough for mixing. So, unless you have a set of good quality external speakers rigged up you'll need the headphones for mixing as well.

Your biggest problem however is likely to be latency. Because the audio is travelling through the computer's circuitry before it's outputted there will inevitably be a short time lag between what you play and when you hear it back. The problem is nothing like as bad as it used to be – before OS X and Core Audio – but even so, without an audio interface with direct monitoring features, you may experience problems. Generally speaking, the faster the computer the lower the latency. Having said all that, if you're just sketching out songs that you intend to record again anyway and you're prepared to live with such issues – who cares? You're being productive and after all, isn't that why you bought a Mac in the first place?

Another cost effective way of recording is to use a Griffin iMic, an inexpensive USB adapter. Because it supports both mic and line level input, you can use it to connect both microphones and instruments to your Mac. Also, because USB isolates the audio signal from any noisy electronics in your computer, you'll get marginally better sound quality.

The audio line in jack is also suitable for recording electrical instruments that output a line level signal, such as synthesisers and sound modules. You can also use it to record your guitar. But there is a problem. Electric guitars use 1/4-inch size instrument cables and because the Mac audio input is 1/8-inch mini-jack, as with the mic, you'll need an adaptor.

The simplest and probably the cheapest solution to the problem is to buy the Griffin GarageBand Guitar Cable. Just plug one end into your guitar and the other into your Mac and it splits the mono guitar signal into the stereo mini-jack. The cable is around 3 metres long.

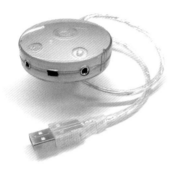

Figure 2.2
The iMic USB adapter can be used to connect guitars and microphones to Apple Macs

Figure 2.3
The GarageBand Guitar Cable – just plug one end into your guitar and the other end into your Mac

Figure 2.4
Monster iStudioLink can be used to plug, mics, guitars and keyboards into your Mac

Alternatively, you could buy the Monster iStudioLink, a simple 1/4-inch (female) to 1/8-inch stereo mini-plug (male) adapter (www.monstercable.com). Simply plug your guitar into the female plug and the mini-plug into the Mac's audio jack. This neat little adapter can also be used to connect microphones and keyboards to your Mac.

So you see at its simplest level recording into GarageBand is very affordable (once you've bought the computer that is). For anything other than personal listening though it's worth investing in either a FireWire or USB audio interface. If you've got your sights set on a recording contract or maybe even distributing your songs on the Web, a more professional approach to the job is needed.

USB Audio and MIDI interfaces

To make good quality recordings you need the same kind of audio input and output connections as those found on a professional recording mixer. That means preamps for condenser microphones and high-impedance instrument inputs for connecting guitars and basses. You'll also need direct monitoring facilities for zero latency and a pair of accurate speakers for monitoring your performance and mixing the finished recording. And if you want to access those mouth-watering software instruments included with GarageBand you'll also need a small keyboard and MIDI interface, to play and control them. Sounds like an awful lot of gear to fit on your desktop, doesn't it? Don't worry, it's a lot less complicated than it might appear. In a modern computer music studio equipment such as this can easily be accommodated on a desktop.

M-Audio manufacture great value-for-money USB and FireWire audio interfaces (www.m-audio.com) and their least expensive device the Mobilepre USB was designed for location laptop recording. Of course, it works just as well with desktop computers like the eMac and it's perfectly adequate for recording with GarageBand. In fact, all the audio connections you're likely to need are here including two high impedance instrument inputs and two phantom powered mic inputs. However it doesn't include a MIDI interface. If you want to play GarageBand's software instruments a separate MIDI interface is required.

Generally speaking the Mobilepre USB is an ideal entry-level audio interface but there is a downside; it only supports 16-bit audio. That's not a problem with GarageBand, which only supports 16-bit audio anyway. But if you were to upgrade to more professional audio software such as Logic or Cubase you'd need to buy another audio interface, to take advantage of the 24-bit resolution that these programs offer.

Figure 2.5
The Mobilepre USB, from M-Audio is perfectly suited for recording with GarageBand

Are there any other affordable audio interfaces available? Yes, dozens. Far too many to cover in detail here in fact.

Tascam produce several audio and MIDI interfaces and one of the most interesting, the US-122, happens to be ideally suited for desktop recording with GarageBand. Like the Mobilepre it's a USB device and features all the connectivity needed for a small set-up with two XLR phantom powered mic inputs and two line-level inputs which can be switched to guitar-level (high impedance). Direct monitoring, two line-level outputs and a dedicated headphone socket are also provided.

Figure 2.6
The Tascam US-122 audio/MIDI interface (USB) is ideal for desktop or laptop recording with GarageBand or more advanced audio software such as Logic

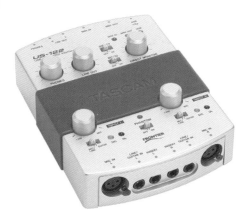

The US-122 scores points over the Mobilepre in a number of areas. To begin with, it supports 24-bit recording (as opposed to 16-bit) which is useful for recording with software other than GarageBand. It also has a MIDI interface, so you can use a keyboard. The most interesting aspect of the US-122 though is the inclusion of analogue inserts, something not often found on small audio interfaces. Using these, you can insert external signal processors like compressors into the recording chain, before the signal reaches your computer. To top it all, Tascam have bundled Cubase LE, a pruned version of Cubase SX.

Yet another reasonably priced USB audio interface is the rugged Edirol UA-25. Its components are housed in a tough aluminium case which makes it an ideal companion to the iBook or PowerBook range. Like the US-122 it supports 24-bit recording, features direct monitoring and a MIDI interface. Two front mounted dual purpose input connections (XLR and 1/4-inch TRS) are suitable for guitars and provide phantom power for condenser microphones. Two left/right outputs provide balanced professional audio (+4dBu) on 1/4-inch jacks. There's also an on-board limiter which will go some way to preventing overloaded signals if you're doing location recording with your laptop.

Figure 2.7
The Edirol UA-25 Audio/MIDI interface features two front mounted input connectors suitable for condenser mics and guitars

FireWire Audio and MIDI interfaces

FireWire devices are more expensive than their USB counterpart but they're more efficient with superior audio transfer rates. If you're a guitarist the FireWire Solo is an ideal way to get started with GarageBand or Logic. Designed from the ground up as an easy-to-use interface for songwriters to record guitars and vocals it features a 1/4-inch guitar input and a professional XLR microphone input on the front

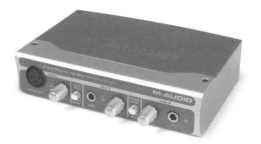

Figure 2.8
The FireWire Solo was designed specially for guitar players

panel. There are also dual line inputs for effects, drum machines and other out-board gear. This model is very much guitar orientated and if you play keyboards you'll need a separate MIDI interface to take advantage of the GarageBand software instruments.

If you're not recording alone and you need more inputs and outputs, including MIDI there are plenty of mid range professional interfaces on the market, far too many to include here in fact. However MOTU (Mark of the Unicorn) have been developing and manufacturing computer music peripherals for the Apple Mac since 1980 and their products are considered by many professionals to be among the best you can buy. The Traveler and the 828mkii are typical examples of the many affordable audio/MIDI interfaces around at the moment that are suitable for beginners and advanced users alike.

Designed for mobile recording but equally at home in the project studio, the Traveler provides four dual mic/instrument inputs, each with individual phantom power (XLR and 1/4-inch TRS), four additional jack inputs and eight analogue audio outputs (balanced/unbalanced 1/4-inch jacks TRS).

The 828mkii is a rack mounted device, more suited to a permanent project studio installation. Although it only has two dual mic/instrument inputs (as opposed to the Traveler's four) it provides another eight 1/4-inch jack inputs; enough in total to record a line-up of guitar, bass, keyboards and drums along with perhaps a guide vocal track. Like the Traveler, it features eight analogue audio outputs in addition to a pair of stereo main outs; a total of 10.

Signal routing and direct monitoring is handled on both models using either CueMix, an on-board software digital mixer, or front panel knobs. Also, if you're working at an advanced level both models include professional features such as SMPTE timecode, S/PDIF in/out, AES/EBU in/out, ADAT optical in/out, ADAT sync port, MIDI in/out and Word clock in/out.

Figure 2.9
With eight analogue inputs and outputs the MOTU Traveler (FireWire) is an ideal audio/MIDI interface for both mobile and project studio recording

And if you need software that's a step up from GarageBand both devices come bundled with AudioDesk, a fully featured software audio workstation for Macs with recording, editing, mixing and real-time 32-bit effects processing facilities. It can be upgraded to AudioDesk 2 or to Digital Performer, MOTU's full-fledged audio and MIDI sequencer.

PCI audio and MIDI interfaces

Although going out of fashion at the lower end of the market since the introduction of FireWire, PCI interfaces are actually quicker at transferring audio than either USB or FireWire devices. They usually take the form of either a breakout box or a set of breakout leads attached to a PCI card. The card itself is inserted into one of the expansion slots found only on the G5 Power Macs.

M-Audio's Delta range covers most studio configurations with their Audiophile cards (4 in/out, MIDI in/out and digital in/out) being the cheapest and their 1010 cards (10 in/out, MIDI in/out, digital in/out and Word Clock) being the most expensive. In fact if you're happy with 24-bit recording with a sampling rate of 96kHz, the world's best selling audio card, the Audiophile 2496 is cheaper now than ever. That's because M-Audio recently added the high-definition Audiophile 192 to their range boasting a 196kHz sampling rate. If you work alone, both of these cards are an excellent choice although you will need either a small mixer such as the Spirit Notepad or a preamp like M-Audio's Audio Buddy or DMP3 to connect up guitars and microphones.

Figure 2.10
The Audiophile 192 (PCI) audio/MIDI interface provides the basic connections required for a small studio set-up

Keyboard controllers and MIDI interfaces

To use the software instruments included with GarageBand and Logic you'll need a MIDI keyboard and a MIDI interface.

Most of the audio interfaces mentioned so far in this chapter include MIDI in and out ports as part of their spec but if yours doesn't, a simple USB device like the M-Audio Uno or Edirol UM-1X is all that's required.

If you don't already own a keyboard companies like M-Audio, Edirol and Yamaha produce dozens of affordable models. The M-Audio Keystation 49e for example features a velocity sensitive keyboard with pitch bend and modulation controls, a volume control slider, foot pedal connections and also functions as a MIDI interface.

Figure 2.11
The Uno 1-in / 1-out USB MIDI interface

A keyboard like this is perfectly adequate for GarageBand. However, in the long run a slightly more expensive keyboard such as the Edirol PCR-30 may be a better purchase. The keyboard has only 32 keys (as opposed to the Keystation's 49) but it features assignable rotary knobs, faders and buttons which you can use to control all manner of goodies within your audio software. For example you could remotely control Logic's mixers with one of the PCR-30's physical faders or tweak a software instrument's parameters with a real knob instead of using a mouse.

Figure 2.12
The M-Audio Keystation 49e is an ideal MIDI keyboard for playing GarageBand's software instruments

Figure 2.13
The Edirol PCR-30 MIDI keyboard and controller features assignable knobs and faders for hands-on manipulation of virtual mixers and software instruments within programs like Logic, Cubase and Digital Performer

Microphones

With the exception of the Audiophile 192, all the audio interfaces mentioned so far feature at least one XLR connection and preamp. They were chosen for a good reason; they can be used to connect condenser microphones. They'll accept dynamic microphones too but condenser types are usually chosen for recording vocals and acoustic instruments.

Figure 2.14
Budget priced multi-pattern studio microphones like the Samson C03 are ideal for recording vocals and acoustic instruments in the project studio

If you're only going to buy one microphone get a condenser. Top-of-the-range models are very expensive but these days companies like Samson Audio manufacture excellent budget models. Their CO3 model for example is a multi-pattern condenser mic developed specifically for project studio use.

But why a condenser? A condenser mic (also referred to as a capacitor mic) features a flexible diaphragm and a rigid, electrically charged back-plate, placed closely together. When sound waves hit the diaphragm the distance between the two plates alters, creating an electrical signal which is amplified by an internal battery or an external preamp. Because the diaphragm is super thin and extremely light, condenser mics are very sensitive with a good high frequency response.

In common with the very best studio mics the Samson CO3 can be switched between different pickup patterns; Cardoid, Omni and Figure 8. Cardoid is the most commonly used setting and being unidirectional rejects sounds on either side of the mic in favour of sounds directly in front of it; useful for recording a solo vocalist. The Omni pickup pattern captures sound from all directions; useful for recording ensembles. The Figure 8 pattern picks up sound directly at the front and back of the microphone; useful for duets and backing vocals.

Dynamic mics work on a completely different principle with a diaphragm being fixed to a coil of wire surrounded by a magnetic field. Sound waves hit the diaphragm which vibrates the coil to create an electrical signal. The louder the sound, the more the diaphragm moves and inevitably, the greater the signal.
Dynamic mics are more robust than condenser types and a good one such as the classic Shure SM58 can be used to close-mic just about anything with surprisingly good results.

Headphones and speakers

Last – but by no means least – on our list of essentials for recording on your Mac are the headphones and loudspeakers, necessary for monitoring your performance while recording.

A frequently asked question: Can I use headphones instead of speakers when recording and mixing my music? The answer is yes, but it's not recommended. Headphones are fine for monitoring your performance while you're recording but for mixing the tracks afterwards you need a couple of decent speakers with a flat frequency response. In fact you should buy the best you can afford because accuracy is paramount when mixing. Forget the speakers included with your Mac for anything other than general listening.

Fortunately good budget reference monitors are becoming increasingly common. The Resolv range from Samson Audio for example are good value for money, Three hundred pounds will buy a pair of their Resolv 60a powered speakers which produce a full sound with a transparent mid-range. M-Audio also manufacture reasonably priced reference monitors; the Studiophile range.

If your budget will not stretch to reference monitors, or you haven't the space to accommodate them, Samson's DMS80 Desktop Monitor System may be the answer. Similar in design to a hi-fi set-up, it's comprised of a stereo amplifier and full range speakers developed specifically for use with keyboard set-ups, project studios, and computer multimedia systems.

Figure 2.15
A pair of studio reference monitors like the Samson Resolv 6a will help you create accurate mixes

Figure 2.16
The DMS80 Desktop Monitoring System was designed by Samson for project studio use

Unlike speakers, accurate headphones are not so critical. But there are one or two factors you should take into consideration before purchasing. A closed design is better than an open type. Why? Because when you're overdubbing vocals or whatever, you don't want sound leaking from your 'phones. This can be picked up and recorded along with your performance. It's not the drastic issue that some people make out and can even be quite effective but even so, it's best avoided and can prove problematic when it comes to mixing. A long lead that connects to just one side is also preferable for avoiding entanglement with instruments and so on. As well as being powerful and comfortable to wear, the AKG K55 studio headphones fit the bill. They're also very reasonably priced.

Figure 2.17
These AKG K55 headphones are a closed-back design, just what you need for zero leakage when overdubbing vocals and so on

Audio MIDI Setup (AMS)

Before using an audio interface you'll need to configure the input and output connections in the OS X Audio MIDI Setup (AMS).

1 Install any drivers that came with your equipment.
2 Ensure that your audio interface is connected to your Mac.
3 Open the AMS. You'll find it under Applications > Utilities > Audio MIDI Setup.

Figure 2.18

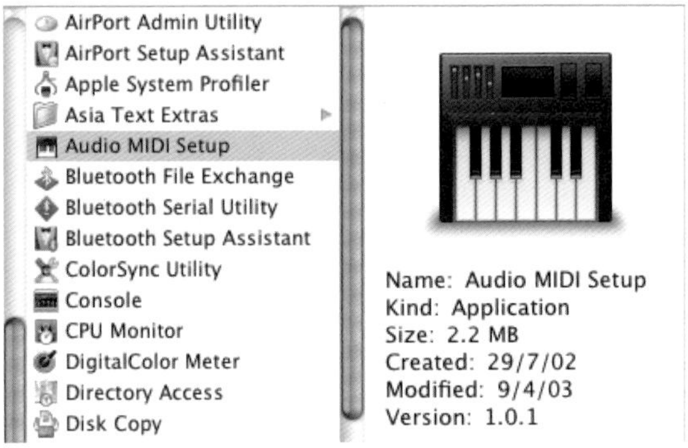

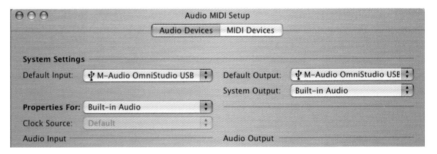

4 Select the Audio Devices tab at the top of the dialogue box.
5 In the System Settings area, select your audio interface in the Default Input pop-up menu. If you don't have a third-party audio interface and you're going to use the audio-in jack on your Mac, choose Built-in Audio.

Figure 2.19

6 By way of a check, open the OS X Sound System Preferences as well and select the Input page. Your device will appear here too (along with any other audio devices you have connected). In fact both the Sound and AMS windows interact. Change the settings in one window and the settings will be reflected in the other. If you're going to use your Mac's analogue audio inputs ensure that Line In is selected in the Sound window.

Figure 2.20

7 In the AMS window, select your audio interface in the Default Output pop-up
   menu. Leave the System Output set to Built-in audio controller. That way you'll
   not hear the system bleeps through your audio interface but through your
   computer's speaker(s).

Before using your MIDI devices you'll need to configure a setup in the OS X Audio
MIDI Setup (AMS).

1 Install any drivers that came with your equipment.
2 Ensure that your MIDI interface is connected to your Mac.
3 Open the AMS. You'll find it under Applications > Utilities > Audio MIDI
   Setup.
4 All connected MIDI devices will show up here (the greyed-out IAC driver
   enables you to configure different setups for different applications). If their
   drivers have been installed correctly, other unconnected devices will also
   appear here (but like the IAC, they'll be greyed out).
5 To add a MIDI keyboard controller (or any other MIDI device) click the Add
   Device icon. A new external device icon appears.
6 Click on the new device's output and and drag a virtual cable to the MIDI
   interface's input.

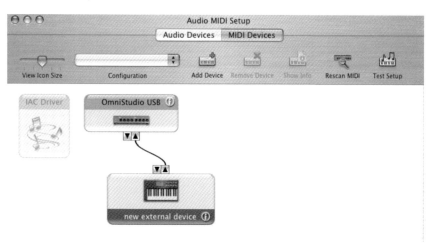

Figure 2.21

Making Music with GarageBand

G arageBand is a brilliantly simple, all-in-one multitrack audio recorder, MIDI sequencer and loop based composition tool. And because it features such an intuitive interface, you don't require a degree in music technology to figure out how to use it. However, like a lot of music software these days, it doesn't come with a printed manual. But if you do get stuck there's a clearly written set of on-line help files. To regurgitate those files here would be pointless. Instead we'll examine the program from a productive perspective and help you with getting started, building arrangements, recording guitars and vocals, using Apple Loops and software instruments, adding effects and mixing.

GarageBand as a multitrack audio recorder

Before programs like GarageBand existed the recording industry used multitrack reel-to-reel tape recorders to record live music. The sound waves produced by musical instruments and singers were captured with microphones, converted to electrical signals and stored on magnetic tape. Different instruments were assigned to different tracks. When the recording was complete it was mixed down to 2-track stereo tape.

Recording with GarageBand is a similar process to old fashioned tape recording but instead of the sound waves being captured on magnetic tape, they're sampled and stored as digital code on your Mac's hard drive (the data is subsequently displayed as a sound wave on an audio track). And instead of mixing the tracks down to 2-track stereo tape you export them to iTunes as stereo digital audio files. Basically, that's how most professional recording is done these days, usually with the aid of an Apple Mac computer running ProTools or Logic software.

Figure 3.1
Digital audio recorded onto four Real Instrument tracks in GarageBand

Figure 3.2
Sound is sampled and stored as digital code on your Mac's hard drive then displayed as a sound wave on a GarageBand Real Instrument track

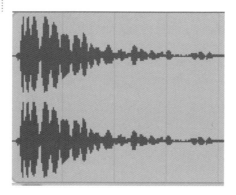

The original GarageBand only allowed you to record one track at a time. For example, you couldn't mic up an entire band and record each instrument onto separate tracks, in a single pass. But that's now changed and with GarageBand 2 you can record up to eight audio tracks and one software instrument in a single pass. But the majority of GarageBand users will probably be working alone. recording their music one track at a time, using a technique called overdubbing. For this type of recording, GarageBand is just the ticket.

Starting with an Apple loop as a basic drum pattern, you can overdub bass, guitar and vocal parts and build up a song, track by track. You can also experiment with the song structure by cutting and pasting segments (regions) of the audio about, until you achieve a cohesive arrangement. In GarageBand, audio tracks are referred to (rather confusingly) as Real Instrument tracks.

GarageBand as a sequencer

Today's recording software began life in the 1980s, as MIDI only applications. At that time the average computer didn't possess the necessary processing power required to handle audio recording. However, they could manage MIDI data and because musicians and recording engineers were already using them, the software developers modelled their sequencing programs on multitrack tape recorders. But instead of audio tracks they had MIDI tracks.

The familiar tape recorder style interface proved popular and MIDI sequencing took off in a big way. For the first time, musicians could record their synthesiser performances as data (not audio) onto MIDI tracks. On playback, the sequencer transmitted the recorded information back to the instrument it was originally played on. In other words, the computer was now controlling the synthesiser. If a wrong note had been played the musician simply corrected it, by editing the data on the MIDI track. Recording it again for the sake of a single mistake was no longer necessary.

By the mid 90s computers were much more powerful and sequencing software programs were running audio and MIDI tracks simultaneously. It was around this time that software instruments first appeared. This was another giant leap forwards because musicians could now record onto MIDI tracks and control software synthesisers as an alternative to routing the data back to their hardware instruments. These days the major sequencers such as Logic and Cubase include a comprehensive set of software instruments with their applications which can be used as plugins. And so does GarageBand.

Info

When they first appeared. MIDI sequencers revolutionised the way music was composed and recorded. Musicians could now record complete songs onto virtual 16-track tape recorders which enabled them to record verses and choruses into patterns and assemble them in what ever order they liked. The finished songs, although conventional in structure, often had a robotic feel to them. In the mid 80s this method of writing gave birth to a whole new style of music known as Synth Pop; think Depeche Mode and Pet Shop Boys.

It may be an entry level program but as a sequencer GarageBand operates just like the big boys and includes an abundant collection of software instruments – basses, guitars, synths and so on – that can be controlled from a MIDI track. In GarageBand, MIDI tracks are called Software Instrument tracks and just like any other sequencer, you can use them to record your performance using a MIDI keyboard and edit the data afterwards.

However, unlike most sequencing software, GarageBand cannot relay the recorded data to any external hardware synthesisers that you might own. To do that, you'll need to upgrade to a sequencer like Logic or Cubase. Editing MIDI data on a Software Instrument track (MIDI track) is also restricted but for general song writing and entry level sequencing there are just enough features to produce the goods.

Figure 3.3
MIDI data recorded onto three Software Instrument tracks in GarageBand

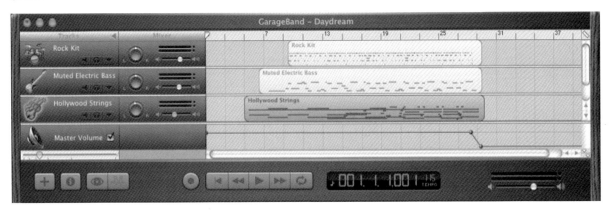

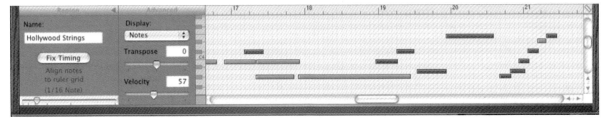

GarageBand as a loop production tool

Figure 3.4
You can examine and edit MIDI note data in GarageBand's Track Editor, where it's displayed graphically, on a grid

When sequencers first appeared, musicians were presented with a wealth of production techniques, previously impossible with just a tape recorder. One of the most obvious was the facility to record a section of music into a MIDI track and loop it repeatedly, for as long as necessary. In the right hands, this technique can be used to compose and produce exciting, rhythmically driven, electronic dance music. It takes many forms with 'techno' and 'house' perhaps being the best known.

Once sequencers were capable of recording audio as well as MIDI data, it wasn't long before dance music producers were importing pre-recorded audio files and looping them alongside their MIDI tracks. But of course, unless the imported audio files had been recorded at an identical speed to that of the song they were working on, the two types of track data would be out of sync. The obvious answer was to time stretch (or shrink) and pitch shift the audio files. It could be done in a conventional sequencer but the process was far from easy.

So, in response to the growing popularity of loop based music production, a few years ago several 'audio only' sequencers appeared on the market. Products such as Ableton Live provided instant time stretching facilities for mixing and matching audio samples regardless of their individual pitch and tempo. Several other audio sequencers such as Fruity Loops and Acid (now Adobe Audition) did much the same thing. These easy-to-use sequencers were, and still are, extremely popular and attracted a whole new generation to computer music making. But until recently these programs lacked MIDI functionality and couldn't run MIDI tracks alongside the audio loops. Now, most of them do – and so does GarageBand.

GarageBand comes with over a thousand Apple Loops; pre-recorded, ready to play performances, by professional musicians. These loops are great way to kick start a new song and particularly useful for creating rhythm tracks. As you add the loops to a composition they're automatically matched to the song's tempo and key, regardless of the pitch and tempo of the original performance. Finding suitable loops is easy too because they're organised by instrument, style and genre. You audition them first, in a loop browser, select those you like and drag and drop them onto an existing track or a blank space on the timeline. GarageBand creates a new track for each loop you add to the timeline.

Figure 3.5
Apple Loops are located and auditioned in the Loop Browser

Loops	Instruments	Acoustic Bass	Name	Tempo	Key	Beats
All	Acoustic Bass	Acoustic Bass (65)	Cool Upright Bass 01	120	C	16
By Genres	Acoustic Guitar	Acoustic (65)	Cool Upright Bass 02	120	C	16
By Instruments	Banjo	Bass (65)	Cool Upright Bass 03	120	C	16
By Moods	Bass	Cheerful (17)	Cool Upright Bass 04	120	C	16
Favorites	Beats	Clean (65)	Cool Upright Bass 05	120	C	8
	Bell	Dark (14)	Cool Upright Bass 07	120	C	8
			Cool Upright Bass 08	120	C	8

Scale: Any   65 items

Quick start, with loops

As mentioned earlier, GarageBand is very intuitive to use and everything you need to know is explained in the online help files. In fact the tutorial (Learn About GarageBand) is very thorough. Nevertheless, it's quite time consuming to wade through, particularly if you know nothing about time signatures and so on. What follows here is a kind of jump start to creating a song, using GarageBand as a loop production tool.

When you start GarageBand it always opens the last song that was open. But you've probably been experimenting with GarageBand already so:

1 Press Command-N, for a new file. When you create a new song GarageBand asks you to name and save it (Figure 3.6). The default location is the GarageBand folder, on your hard drive. Before you can go further, GarageBand also needs to know the tempo, the time signature and the key signature of your song. If you're not sure what all this means leave the default settings in place, just for now.

A new song contains a single Software Instrument track named Grand Piano by default.

2 Press Command-L, to open the loop browser and find the 'Blue Jazz Piano 02'

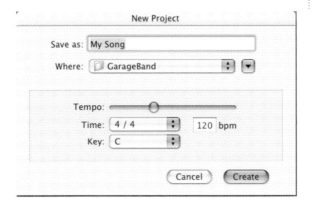

Figure 3.6
name and save your new song

loop. There are several routes but choosing By Genres > Jazz > Piano will get you there.

3 Select the loop and drag it onto the Grand Piano track, placing it at the very beginning of bar 1. Once on the timeline, loops become regions. You'll notice that the region spans four bars.

Press C, to cycle the loop. Save the song.

Figure 3.7

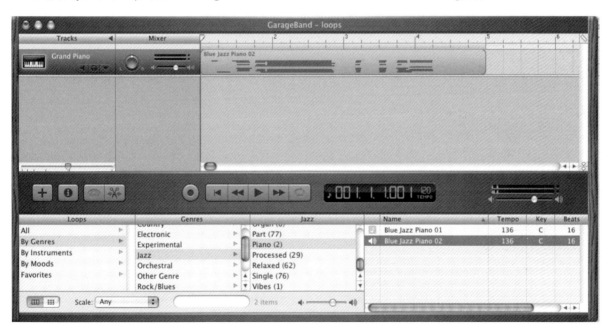

If you can't hear any sound when you audition or play the loop:

4 Open GarageBand's preferences, click the Audio/MIDI tab and ensure that the audio outputs are correct. If you have an audio interface connected to your computer it appears here, in the pop-up menu, alongside the built-in audio controller. Any other MIDI devices you have connected will also show up here.

Info

o audition a loop in the browser, click on it once. Click again, to turn it off

Figure 3.8
Click the Audio/MIDI tab and ensure that the audio outputs are correct.

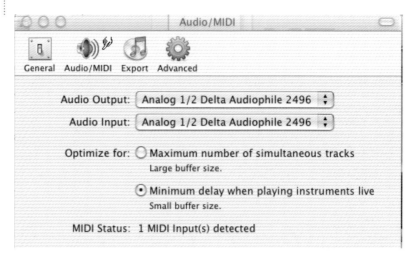

Okay, that's a cool sounding piano. But it needs some rhythm behind it:

5   Find the loop named Funky Latin Drums 01 and drag it onto the time line. Don't worry about creating a new track, GarageBand does this for you (keep the cycle region button on and the loop will automatically span four bars, as a region).

Figure 3.9

Ensure that both the regions begin at bar 1 and play them through. What a difference. Things are beginning to liven up.

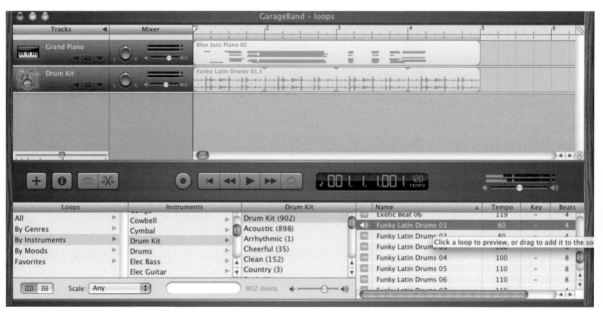

The piano and drums have set up a nice groove but of course, they'll sound even better with the addition of a bass player:

6   Find the loop named Cool Upright Bass 02 and drag it onto the timeline.

GarageBand will create a track called Acoustic Bass (keep the cycle region
button on and the loop will automatically span four bars). Line the new region
up with the other two and play them through.

Figure 3.10

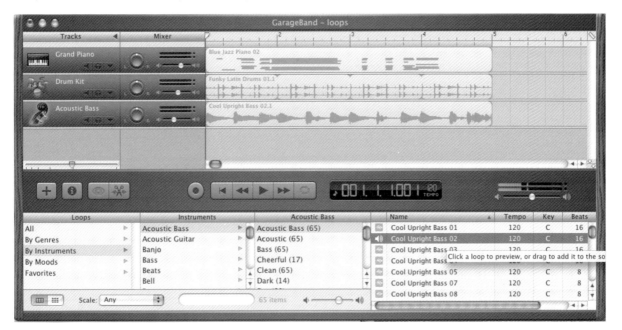

The trio sounds great. Why not make it a quartet?

7   Find the loop named Funky Electric Guitar 07 and drag it onto the timeline,
    alongside the others. Play them through. Quite a tight outfit, don't you think?
    Save the song.

Figure 3.11

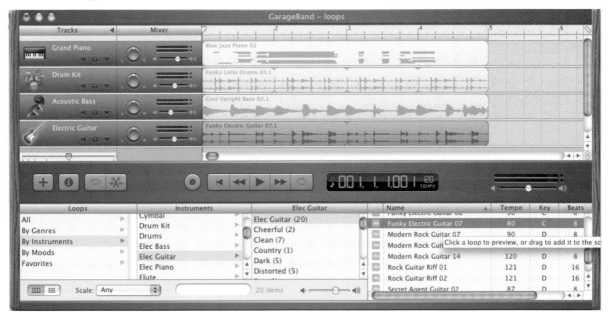

That was easy, wasn't it? You created a four bar sequence in lightning fast time. It sounds great just as it is but there's a lot more you can do with those sounds.

Changing instruments

1 Select track 1 and press Command-I, to open the Track Info window. You'll see that it's a Software Instrument track. The window is divided into two sections. Instrument categories are listed on the left. Individual instruments are listed on the right. At the moment the list reads: Pianos and Keyboards > Grand Piano.
2 Choose the Whirly piano instead. GarageBand will rename the track Whirly and switch to a cool electric piano sound.
3 Play the sequence, to hear the difference While the song is playing, try out a few more pianos. You don't necessarily have to stop GarageBand every time.

So how come the track can play different pianos? Because, in GarageBand, a Software Instrument track is really a MIDI track. The recorded notes (MIDI data) are playing back a Software Instrument as opposed to a Real Instrument.

Tip

Use the spacebar, on your computer, to start and stop GarageBand. If the Track Info window is open, it will float.

Figure 3.12

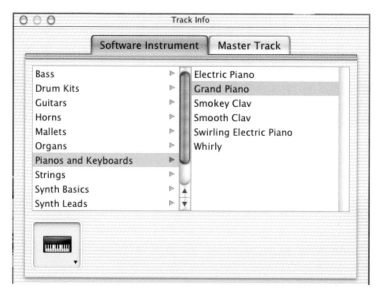

Tip

To listen to a track by itself, click on its Solo button (the headphone icon in the track's header).

4 Now select the Electric Guitar track and open the Track Info window. You'll notice that, this time, it's a Real Instrument track. What you heard here was an audio recording of a musician playing a real guitar. The window is divided into two halves. On the left is a list of instrument categories. On the right is a list of individual instruments. Near the bottom are channel input settings which, for the moment, you can ignore.
5 From the lists, select Guitar > Acoustic Guitar Echoes and play the track (you'll be asked by GarageBand to name and save your current settings – save them as Electric Guitar). Of course, what you are now hearing is not really another instrument but the same audio recording of a guitar being treated with echo

effects. More on those later. For now, just have fun experimenting with the different pre-sets on the list.

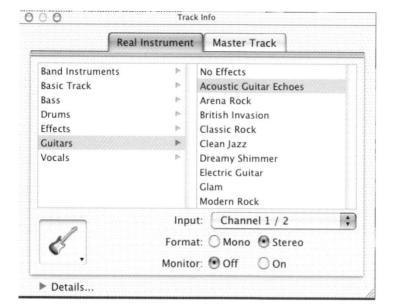

Figure 3.13

To return to the original track select Electric Guitar from the instrument list (you've just named it, remember?)

Extending a song by looping and moving regions

Basically, what you've done so far is discover how GarageBand works as a loop production tool. But of course, four bars of music is ludicrously short and, at this tempo, lasts for only 6 seconds! Fortunately loop based music is repetitive by nature and extending this composition is a simple matter of looping and moving regions.

To loop a region: Grab its upper right-hand corner (the cursor becomes a loop pointer). Now drag to the right and extend the loop as far as necessary.

To move a region: Grab it in the centre or anywhere but the edges and drag it to a new position.

Of course, just looping all four tracks will result in boring monotonous music (a trap that's easily fallen into) so how can you make it interesting? Well, at the moment, all four tracks are playing together, so why not create some spaces?

1 Loop the drum region as far as bar 21.
2 Move the piano region to bar 13 and loop it as far as bar 21.
3 Move the bass region to bar 5 and loop it as far as bar 21.
4 Move the guitar region to bar 9 and loop it as far as bar 21.

Info

Click the note icon in the time display to change reading to absolute time (hrs. min. sec.). Click again to revert to musical time (bars and beats).

Info

How far and where you can move and loop a region is determined by the Snap to Grid setting. Click on the ruler icon to view the settings.

Figure 3.14

Now that's not exactly a revolutionary arranging technique but it has extended the piece to 40 seconds. However to repeat things again, without variation, runs the risk of boring your listeners. What about some funky horns over what is, so far, just a backing track.

> **TIP**
>
> To view large areas of the timeline use the zoom slider (bottom left-hand corner, below the track headers).

5 Loop all four regions as far as bar 37.
6 In the loop browser, find RnB Horn Section 05 and drag it onto the timeline at bar 21. Loop it as far as bar 29.
7 Now find RnB Horn Section 09 and drag it onto the timeline at bar 29. Loop it as far as bar 37.

Figure 3.15
72 seconds of funky music

You now have 72 seconds of funky music that doesn't sound boring for a moment.

So far you've only used GarageBand as a loop production tool, using other people's pre-recorded music. It's time to move on and record some music of your own.

Recording and playing Software Instruments

The most basic method of playing a Software Instrument is to use the GarageBand keyboard (press Command-K, to open it). But it's really only good for auditioning the various software instruments on offer. Playing a piano keyboard with a mouse just isn't practical. To play anything half decent you'll need a proper MIDI keyboard and a MIDI interface of some kind. However, if you don't yet have a MIDI set-up of your own, for now, use GarageBand's on-screen keyboard instead.

Okay, you're now entering the world of MIDI sequencing and all this talk of keyboard playing may be troubling you. Don't worry. It's a common myth that you have to be a good keyboard player to record MIDI tracks. Many accomplished musicians who play instruments such as guitar and saxophone are terrible piano players but that doesn't prevent them recording MIDI tracks with programs like GarageBand. Maybe you already play a musical instrument. If so, you must have encountered fast passages that you couldn't play the first time round. What did you do? Give up? Of course not. You practised them slowly. Only when the difficult bits were under-the-fingers did you speed them up again (at least that's what you should have done).

The same principles apply when you're playing a GarageBand Software Instrument. If you can't play something fast, just slow it down:

1 Press Command-N, for a new file.

This time, before you name and save the new song, use the slider to alter the default tempo, to suit your keyboard playing skills.

If you're an inexperienced musician, set the tempo at 90 bpm or perhaps even slower. You can change this later, if necessary. The time and key signatures can be left at the default settings. When the song opens you'll be presented with a blank Software Instrument track entitled Grand Piano. That'll do nicely. Leave things as they are.

Figure 3.16
You're presented with a blank Software Instrument track entitled Grand Piano.

Figure 3.17

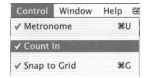

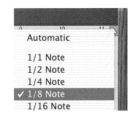

Info

If Snap to Grid is active (use Command-G to turn it on and off) any regions or notes that you move will lock into place according to the grid setting. If it's inactive, you can move things freely.

2 Play a note on your keyboard. If you can't hear anything, check that everything is correct in the OS X Audio MIDI Setup utility. See Chapter 2 page 24 for details.

3 Open GarageBand's preferences (above) and ensure that the metronome is set to click only during recording, not during playback.

4 In the Control menu, activate Count In. While you're there, tick Metronome and Snap to Grid as well.

5 Choose a value for the timeline grid (click on the ruler icon – far right corner, in the beat ruler). 1/8 or 1/16 will do for now.

6 Ensure that the playhead is at bar 1. Press R. Wait for the four beat count-in and play something simple on the keyboard. Do your best to stay in time with the metronome.

7 When you're done, stop the recording and you'll see that GarageBand has created a region on the track. Play it back. If you think that you can do it better…

8 Press Command-D, to clone the track (an identical, empty track is created). Return to the first track and press M, to mute it.

9 Select the second track and record another version. Obviously you can keep recording and comparing versions for as long as you like. When you're finished, keep one track and delete the unwanted versions.

10 Press Command-E, to open the track editor. The notes you played are displayed graphically on a grid. The vertical keyboard, on the left, indicates their pitch.

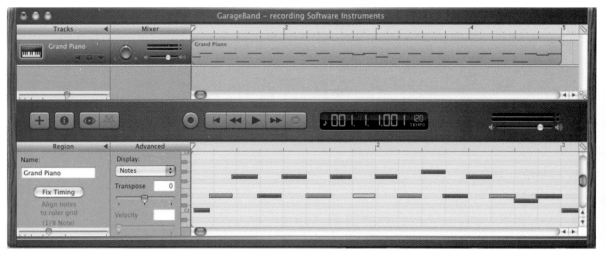

Figure 3.18

11 Using the slider (bottom left-hand corner) zoom in on some of the notes you played. Unless you possess robotic timing, some of them will be displayed either side of the grid positions. They may sound fine but strictly speaking, they're out of time (no offence intended). To remedy the situation, press the Fix Timing button. The notes will move to their nearest grid position. Play the track back, to hear the difference. The result may or may not be closer to how you intended to play. To return to the original timing, press Command-Z.

Figure 3.19 (top)
Notes on the grid before Fix Timing is applied

Figure 3.20 (below)
The same notes, after Fix Timing is applied

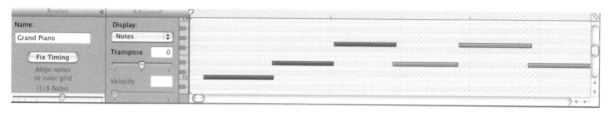

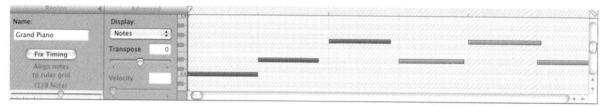

Cycle recording with drum kits

Like all sequencers, GarageBand provides facilities for cycle recording. By setting up a cycle region you can record a region piece by piece, adding something new on each pass. You can do this with all the software instruments but it's probably most useful when compiling a drum track.

Here's how it's done:

1 Create a new song. Choose a comfortable speed. Select a grid setting of 1/8. Ensure the count-in is active.
2 Open the Track Info window and change the default Grand Piano track to a drum kit. Choose any kit you fancy.
3 Press the note C1, on your MIDI keyboard and you'll hear a kick drum sound. Press E1 (two white notes higher) and you'll hear a snare drum.
   Press C (on your computer), to set up a four bar cycle and record a four-to-the-bar kick drum beat (or something similar). When you reach the end of the cycle, stop playing but leave GarageBand in record mode.
4 As the region cycles you can add snare (E1) and hi-hat (F#1), as and when you like. Experiment with cymbal crashes and toms as well, if you want. When you're happy, press the spacebar, to stop recording.
5 Play the region back. If it sounds a bit rough, don't worry; just press the Fix Timing button, in the track editor.

TIP

The fixed timing feature, in the track editor, is a great way to reign in wayward notes. But applying it to an entire region will result in robotic sounding music (fine, if that's what you want). For better results, select just the notes you want to correct.

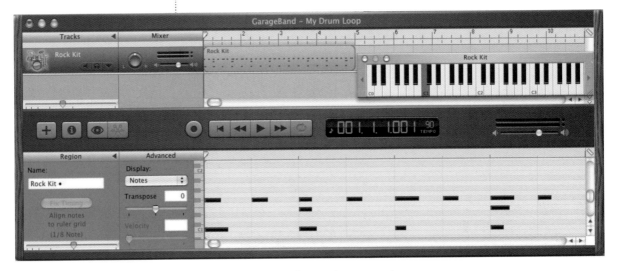

Figure 3.21

Using third party software instruments

You're not just limited to GarageBand's software instruments. If you happen to have any third party Audio Unit instruments on your system you can use those too. Place them in one of the following locations on your Mac:

HD > Library > Audio > Plug-ins > Components
HD > Users > Home > Library > Audio > Components

Now you can load them into GarageBand. Create a new software instrument track, select it and press Command-I, to open the track info window. In the details section, use the Generator pop-up menu to locate and load your third party software instruments.

Figure 3.22

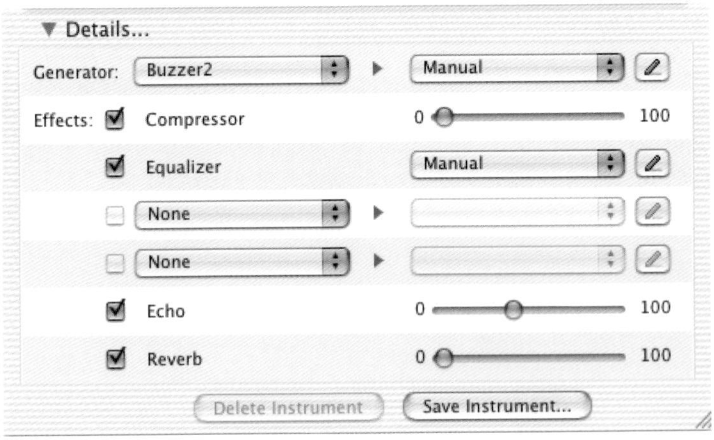

And that's the basics of recording software instruments. You haven't performed any detailed editing or used any of GarageBand's effects but that comes later. It's time to move on to audio recording.

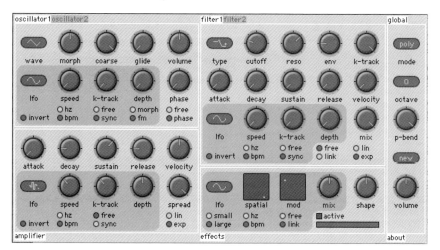

Figure 3.23
If you're looking for a powerful synth to use with GarageBand, go to http://www.alphakanal.de/snipsnap/space/Buzzer2 and download Buzzer2 – it's brilliant

Recording on a Real Instrument track

Open GarageBand's preferences, click the Audio/MIDI tab and ensure that the audio inputs and outputs are correct. If you have an audio interface connected to your computer it appears here, in the pop-up menu, alongside the built-in audio controller. Any MIDI devices you have connected will also show up here.

Before you can record audio you need to create a blank Real Instrument track. So assuming you've already opened a new song:

From the Track menu, select New Basic Track. A brand new audio track appears. Open the track info window and you'll see that this a Real Instrument track. You'll also notice that the track is set to stereo, by default. If you're planning to record a keyboard or another instrument with stereo outputs, leave the stereo setting as it is. The input channels will display 1/2. If you're planning to sing or play a solo instrument such as a guitar, change the setting to mono. What's available in the input setting pop-up depends on whether you're using the Mac's built-in audio or an external audio interface.

If you're using the Mac's audio input, turn the monitor option on. If you're using an external monitoring system via an audio interface or a mixer, turn the monitor option off.

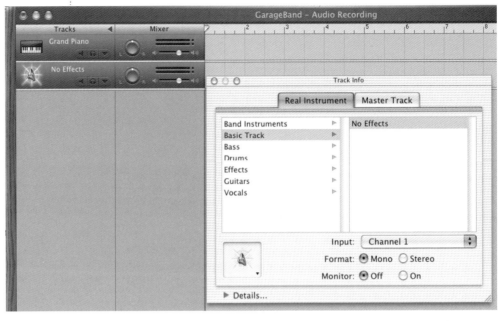

Figure 3.24

- Play your instrument and watch the track meter. Adjust the volume of your instrument so that you have the highest possible signal level without going into the red.
- Decide on a tempo. Unlike Apple loops, audio that you record yourself cannot be time-stretched to fit another tempo. So think hard about this before you begin recording.
- Last minute checks: Ensure the metronome is turned on and the count-in is active.
- Press R, to record, wait for the count-in to pass and 'play that thing'. As you record your instrument a new region is created, behind the playhead, containing an audio waveform.
- Play back the audio region you've just recorded and examine the waveform in the track editor.

Figure 3.25

And basically, that's how you record an Real Instrument track (audio track). Audio editing is limited in GarageBand although you can cut, copy, paste and delete sections. More on that later. It's time to record another track but this time you'll add effects.

Recording with effects

Your first audio track was created without effects. However, GarageBand also gives you the option to hear your performance through an effects setting, as you play or sing. For example, if you're a singer, a touch of reverb will flatter your voice, make you feel more relaxed and help you turn in a better performance than if you just heard your voice dry (think, singing in the bathroom). It doesn't matter how much or how little reverb you use because only the dry, untreated performance is recorded. The wet, treated voice is for monitoring purposes only.

Of course, you can treat instruments with effects as you record, in the same way as vocals:

1   To create a new track press Option-Comand-N (Track > New Track) and choose the Real Instrument option in the New Track window.
2   From the left-hand column, choose a category for your instrument or voice.
3   The effects settings, in the right-hand column, contains a set of effect presets, for the chosen instrument or voice. Choose something suitable. In the example below, British Invasion, a guitar amp effect has been selected.
4   Select your input and turn on the monitor (to hear the effect as you perform).

Figure 3.26

5 To begin with, just play along with the first track. When you're ready, record this track in same way that you recorded the first one.
6 Play back the song. You'll now hear the instrument or recorded voice with the effect of your choice. You can change this to another effect, using the track info window, anytime you like. The illustration below shows two completed Real Instrument tracks.

Figure 3.27

And that, basically, is how you use GarageBand as a multitrack audio recorder. But what if you've made a mistake and you don't relish the idea of recording an entire track all over again? Punch-in and punch-out recording is the answer.

Punching in and out using cycle record

At its simplest, punch-in and punch-out recording can be done manually but it's not an easy operation if you're working alone. It's better to automate the process using cycle record:

1 Ensure that the count-in and metronome are turned on.
2 Set up a cycle that encompasses the audio you want to replace. Remember, the grid setting is directly related to the playhead position, so adjust it accordingly.
3 Press record and play after the count-in. GarageBand will start recording at the beginning of the cycle and stop recording at the end. Unlike when you cycle record on a Software Instrument track, this time, instead of merging old and new material, GarageBand erases the existing audio and replaces it with your newly recorded material. The cycle continues (you'll hear your new material) until you press stop. The result will look something like this:

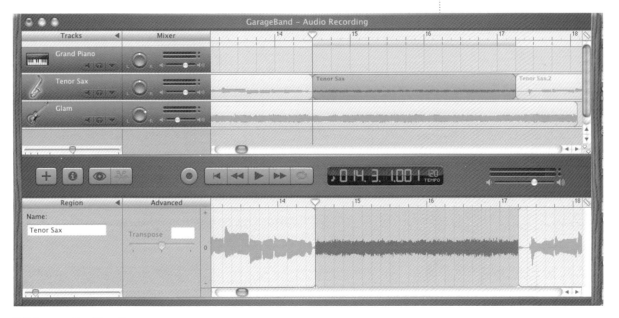

Editing on the Timeline

Figure 3.28

Earlier in this chapter you began arranging a song by looping and moving regions about on the timeline. You can of course take this a stage further by cutting, copying and pasting them as well. The edit menu contains the relevant functions. But what if you want to move or copy just a part of a region? Just split it in two:

1   Select the region(s) and move the playhead to the point where you need to make a split.
2   Press Command-T, to divide the region into two sections (they will be numbered 1 and 2).

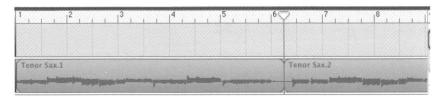

The new region can now be moved, deleted or copied to another location using cut and paste. To paste the region in the correct place, move the playhead to the point in the timeline where you want the region to start.

Just as you may want split regions you may also want to join them together. It's a simple matter of selecting the regions and pressing Command-J. You can only join together regions of the same type and can't, for example, join up Software Instruments and Real Instrument regions. Neither can you join Apple Loops together.

Editing notes in the Track Editor

While the structure of a piece of music can be edited on the timeline, detailed editing of a region's contents can only be carried out in the track editor. You obtained a glimpse of this, earlier in this chapter (under the heading Recording and Playing Software Instruments) when you used the Fix Timing feature. It's time to examine the track editor in more detail and to explore some it's creative and corrective possibilities.

When you open the track editor with a Software Instrument region selected the MIDI data is always displayed graphically, on a piano roll style grid. Pitch is represented vertically (piano keyboard, on the left-hand side) and time horizontally (the beat ruler, above the grid). Four types of data can be displayed on this grid which you select from the Display pop-up menu, in the Advanced section.

When Notes is selected (default setting), any notes you've played can be seen on the grid. How they are displayed is determined by the grid selection you make, which is independent from the timeline's grid settings. As you know already, the timing can be fixed (quantised) according to the grid setting and is a handy feature for bringing inaccurately played notes into line. But it can also be used creatively, to inject swing into jazzier styles of music. To hear the effect: Record a few 1/8 notes, choose a grid setting of 1/8 Swing Heavy (or Light), select the entire region and press Fix Timing.

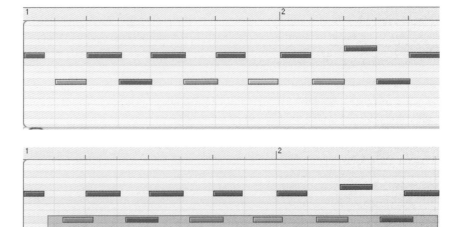

Figure 3.29
Notes in the Track Editor before applying Swing

Figure 3.30
Notes in the Track Editor after Swing is applied – every other 1/8 note is moved to the right (played back slightly later)

Changing a note's length

You can alter the length of notes (or groups of notes, using Shift) on the grid by dragging their ends, to the right. To alter the pitch of an entire region, firstly select it in the timeline and then use the Transpose slider, in the track editor. It has a range of three octaves up and down, either side of zero.

Changing a note's pitch

To alter the pitch of a note (or groups of notes, using Shift) all you need do is drag the note(s) up or down on the grid.

Tip

If you alter the notes in a looped region, all instances of the loop will be changed as well. If this is not want you want to do, use the split command to isolate just the notes you intend altering.

Changing a note's volume
You can alter the volume of individual notes (or groups of notes, using Shift) with the velocity slider. The value (1-127) reflects how hard a note is struck on the keyboard.

Editing MIDI controller data in the Track Editor

Three types of MIDI controller can be recorded and edited in Garage Band: modulation (think vibrato), pitch bend (think note bending on a guitar or wind instruments) and sustain (the same effect as holding down a piano's sustain pedal – the notes ring on). To record this data you need a MIDI controller. You can't do it with GarageBand's on-screen keyboard. Pitch bend and modulation are transmitted using a controller wheel, commonly found on synths and MIDI keyboards. You select the type from the Display pop-up menu, in the Advanced section.

When Pitchbend is selected any pitch bend data that you recorded is displayed on the grid as an envelope. Anything above zero raises the pitch. Anything below zero lowers the pitch. You can alter the curve by selecting and dragging the nodes.

Figure 3.30

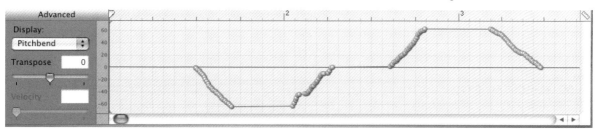

When Modulation is selected any modulation data that you recorded is displayed on the grid as an envelope. Modulation is represented numerically (0-127). The higher the value, the more intense the effect.

Figure 3.31

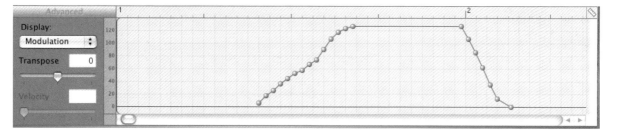

When Sustain is selected a single node represents either on or off. In the picture below sustain is turned on in bar 1 and is turned off at bar 2.

Figure 3.32

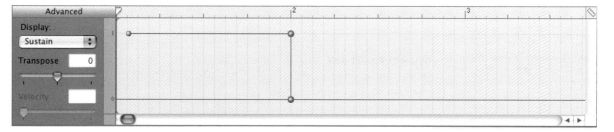

Audio editing in the Track Editor

To be honest there's not much you can do by way of audio editing in the track editor that can't be achieved in the timeline. But you do get a magnified view of a region's waveform which means you can work more accurately.

Figure 3.33

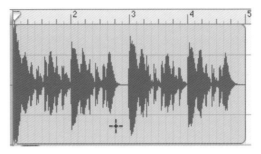

To split a waveform, you select a portion of it, using the crosshair pointer (it replaces the normal mouse pointer). Then you click on the selected portion, to create a new region. In the picture below one region is divided into three regions, each with a new name. You can move, resize and loop the new region(s) in the normal way. If the original waveform had its origins in an Apple Loop you can also transpose the region(s) using the slider, located in the advanced section of the track editor.

Figure 3.34

In the original GarageBand you could only transpose audio waveforms originating from Apple Loops and not audio that you recorded yourself. But now, with its enhanced tuning and timing features, GarageBand 2 provides tools to fix out of tune notes and tighten up the timing of recorded audio.

Mixing – automating volume

When you've finished the writing, arranging, recording and editing of your songs the next step is to mix all your individual tracks down to two track stereo. Unlike a full-fledged production package GarageBand doesn't have a dedicated mixer page.

Instead, a simple track mixer containing volume and pan control is provided. If you can't see it, click on the triangle, in the topmost track header. The volume slider is self-explanatory. Move it to the right and the volume increases.

Mixing manually with a software mixer is much more difficult than with a hardware unit because you can only address one track at a time. Using a hardware mixer you can use two hands and make fine adjustments very quickly. To overcome this problem, full-fledged music software production programs such as Logic provide extensive automation features which enable you to pre-program all aspects of a mix including pan and effects. In GarageBand you're limited to automating just the volume. But that's fine because volume is the most important and most used parameter in the average mix anyway.

Every track has a hidden volume curve. To see it, click on the triangle next to the Solo button in the track's header. In its unaltered state, the volume curve appears below the track in the timeline as a horizontal line extending the length of the track. Raise the track's volume with the slider and the curve moves up. Reduce the track's volume and the curve moves down. To activate the curve, tick the check-box in the curve's header.

Figure 3.35

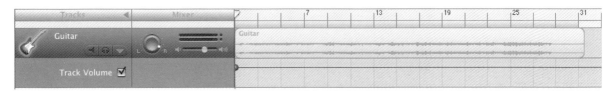

By clicking on the line you can create control points. These can be dragged up or down to create volume changes at specific points in the timeline. In the screenshot below, a simple fade-out has been created towards the end of the region.

Figure 3.36

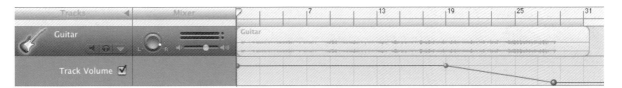

Mixing – pan control

To the left of the volume slider you'll find a knob to control the panning of the track. Rotate the knob fully to the left and you'll hear sound only in the left speaker. Rotate it to the right and you'll hear sound in just the right speaker. With the knob In its centre position the track volume is dispersed equally between the left and right speakers. Placing the knob slightly left or right of centre will increase the volume on each side respectively.

You can use this pan control creatively by placing different track's and their instruments at different positions in the stereo field. There are no hard and fast rules about where exactly to place instruments but there are conventions which, to begin with anyway, you are advised to adhere to. Vocals are usually placed in centre, for balance and clarity. Bass guitar usually goes in the centre along with the snare and kick drum. The remainder of the drum kit is panned right and left according to the physical layout of the kit. Where the other instruments are placed is not quite so important. As general guide, place them as they would appear on a concert platform; keyboards slightly to left and guitar to the right perhaps. Aim for an even balance with the overall volume distributed equally on either side. Keep a watch on the master level meters (bottom right-hand corner of GarageBand's user interface).

Of course many of the Real Instrument Apple Loops that come with GarageBand are pre-recorded in stereo anyway and leaving them dead centre will usually suffice.

The screenshot below shows the stereo panning in Daydream, one of GarageBand's demos. Drums and cymbals are in the centre along with bass guitar. So too are the strings and horns. But to create interest, the guitar is panned hard right and the piano is way off to the left. The synth is also placed left (but not as far as the piano).

Figure 3.37
Stereo panning in Daydream, one of GarageBand's demos

Mixing – adding track effects

Once your track volumes and pan positions are sorted out it's time to consider whether any of the instruments require effects treatment. As you've probably discovered, many of GarageBand's instruments come with pre-configured effects settings, individually tailored to suit the instrument in question. But on mixdown things can sound very different when listened to as a whole and some of them may require adjustment. Fortunately, when you record with GarageBand's effects turned on the audio itself remains dry. You can change the settings at anytime prior to the stereo mixdown so you're free to experiment.

To access the effects on a Real Instrument track press Command-I, to open the Track Info window, and click on the Details tab. The effects and their parameter settings are contained in the lower drop-down section.

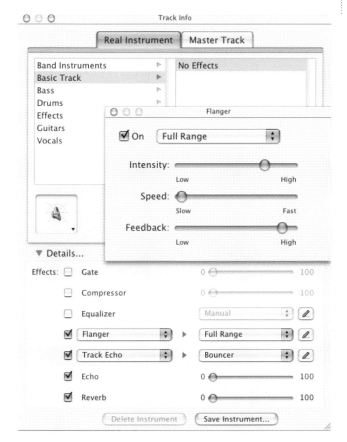

Figure 3.38

The effects on a GarageBand track follow a set order. The first three – gate, compressor and equaliser – are permanently available and simply turned on and off. These are followed by two blank slots where you can select other GarageBand effects plus any third party Audio Unit processors installed on your Mac. All five effects are known as 'insert' effects and are track specific.

And how do you use these insert effects? Basically, however you like. Anything goes, as long as it works. Having said that, just like the pan settings, rules of thumb and conventions do exist. To begin with at least, you'd be wise to follow them. Here's a run down on the effects available in GarageBand and a few pointers on how to use them.

Gate

A noise gate (sometimes called an expander) removes unwanted noises during gaps in the audio. When the input level falls below a predetermined threshold the gate reduces the gain. In other words, when a track's instrument stops playing for a moment the gate kicks in and turns down the volume. Any noise you or your instrument might have made when you ceased playing – rustling lyric sheets, guitar hums and crackles, foot-tapping, knocking over the mic stand (only joking), even breathing – can be removed during the pause.

To use GarageBand's gate, slowly move the slider to the right until any unwanted noise on the track disappears. If the gate begins chopping off notes and vocal syllables move the slider back a little.

Compressor

A compressor works as an automatic volume control, turning down the volume when the audio is too loud and turning it up when it's too quiet. Why should you need that?

Suppose you've recorded a vocal and, on listening back, you discover that your voice varied considerably in volume over the course of the song. The high notes were sung more vigourously and as a result, were recorded louder. They tend to leap out of the mix. The lower notes were sung with less intensity and the recorded signal is rather low. They tend to get buried in the mix. You could, of course, ride the faders (constantly adjust them while you're mixing), to obtain an even signal. But that's a difficult task even on a hardware console, let alone using a mouse in GarageBand. You could also set up an automated volume curve but finding and rectifying all the uneven spots is a time consuming task.

A compressor does all this for you, automatically. When the input level exceeds a predetermined threshold the compressor reduces the gain. When the input signal is below the threshold, it's unaffected.

Compression is also used creatively, to beef up guitar, bass and drums in rock music. Dance music producers also use heavy doses of compression on bass and drums, to get that floor-quaking effect.

GarageBand's compressor is very simple to operate. Just use the slider to increase the compression effect.

Equalizer

Equalisation (EQ) is a fancy term for tone control. You use it in the same way that you use the treble and bass controls on the average hi-fi unit. But in GarageBand you use it on a track-by-track basis to balance the high, low and midrange frequencies of individual instruments and vocals. To get started, choose a preset from the pop-up menu.

You can cut or boost bass and treble frequencies using a single slider. The midrange frequencies are adjustable. Using a second slider, you firstly select a spe-

Figure 3.39
The Equalizer pop-up menu.

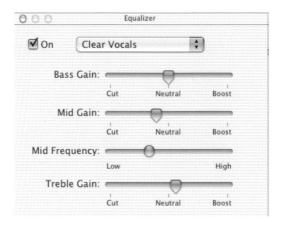

cific frequency, between the lows and highs, before cutting and boosting the signal in the normal way.

Bass and Treble reduction

These two effects are extremely useful when mixing. Technically speaking they're known as lowpass and highpass filters. In other words they're used to let certain frequencies through while rejecting others. The bass reduction tool (lowpass filter) cuts frequencies above a specified point, determined with the slider. Use it to reduce muddiness at the low end of your mixes, often caused by two sounds competing for the same frequencies; bass and drums perhaps. In a dance track it might even be two drum loops that are competing for space.

Vocals too can suffer from booming, as a result of the singer moving in too close to the microphone. Rather than repeat what might otherwise be a great take, use the bass reduction tool to shave the enhanced bass frequencies (known as the proximity effect).

The treble reduction tool works in the same way but cuts frequencies below the specified frequency.

Tip

Try to use EQ correctively, to bring out a particular element (a vocal perhaps) of a recording that might otherwise be buried in the mix.

Tip

Cutting a frequency is usually better than trying to boost it. You want to hear more highs? Try cutting the lows first (before boosting the highs).

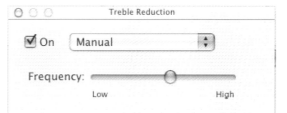

Figure 3.40
Bass and treble reduction tools.

That's the more conventional processors 'done and dusted'. On to the more esoteric signal processors in GarageBand's arsenal.

Distortion and Overdrive

These are guitar derived effects. If you need to crunch-up your guitar, or anything else for that matter, you can use these tools to do it. Distortion will provide you with the sound of wrecked speakers (without the expense of actually ruining your amp) and Overdrive will provide a similar effect but warmer and more musical. Apart from guitar, try them out on drum loops for a nasty industrial effect.

Figure 3.41
Distortion and overdrive

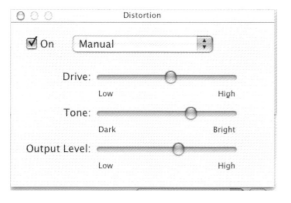
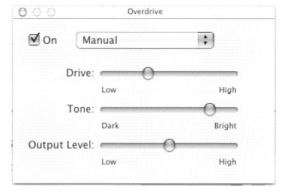

Bitcrusher

A cut down version of Logic's ultimate distortion box. This one's for people who like their music on the nasty side. The resolution slider progressively destroys the pristine 16-bit audio you painstakingly recorded onto your hard-drive. Take it to the limit and hear for yourself! The second slider resamples the audio in real time. Again an effect that's rather difficult to put into mere words. Use it to crunch-up synths, guitars and whatever else takes your fancy. A warning: Bitcrusher can damage your ears when used at high volumes.

Figure 3.42
Bitcrusher can damage your ears when used at high volumes.

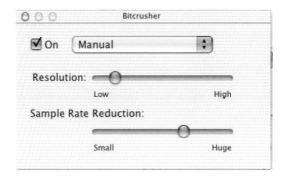

Automatic Filter

Like Bitcrusher, this one's derived from Logic. And like the bass reduction tool, mentioned earlier, it's a lowpass filter but with a couple of extra features. You use the frequency slider to determine the point where the filter kicks in and the resonance slider to emphasise the frequency range at the cut-off point. As you increase the resonance, the filter oscillates. Another warning: don't move it too far otherwise you could damage your ears. You can alter and control the filter sweeps using the intensity slider and control the modulation rates with the speed slider.

Autofilter really is an extremely versatile tool and best understood by examining the various presets. Underwater sounds and wah-wah are specialities of the house. But once again; if you value your eardrums, go easy with the resonance slider!

Figure 3.43
Go easy with this if you value your eardrums!

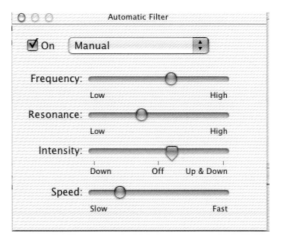

Track Echo

Although echo is available as send effect in GarageBand this one is track specific. The delay time is synced to your song tempo and you use the repeat slider to determine the number of echoes. If you want the echoes to become gradually darker move the colour slider to the left. For progressively brighter echoes, move the slider to the right. Once again, this is an example of lowpass and highpass filtering. Use the intensity slider to control the volume of the repeat echo (not the original signal).

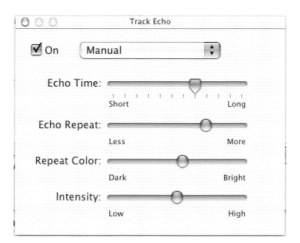

Figure 3.44

Chorus

Probably the most used effect of all time, particularly on guitar. How does it work? The audio signal is split into two signals. One is delayed and subjected to various degrees of pitch modulation before being mixed in with the original, dry signal. GarageBand's chorus is simplicity itself. Use the intensity slider to increase the depth of chorus and the speed slider to alter the modulation rate. It's most effective on polyphonic instruments like guitar or piano and produces a rich, fat, swirling sound.

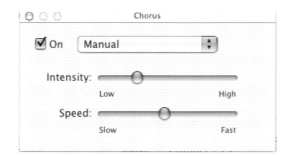

Figure 3.45

Flanger

Very similar to chorus but with an extra control slider for feeding the processed signal back into its own input. In other words the processed audio is processed a second time. The result is an undulating effect, similar in character to the sounds produced by the Automatic Filter. Flanging is typically used on guitar but you can use it on just about anything, even drums.

Figure 3.46

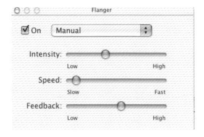

Phaser

Another classic modulation effect, sometimes confused with flanging. GarageBand's phaser controls are identical to the flanger but the effect is smoother, more musical and less metallic.

Figure 3.47

Tremolo

A favourite with guitarists since the 60s, tremolo is achieved by modulating the volume of the signal not its pitch. Simple to use with speed and intensity sliders. As a mono effect it's not particularly spectacular sounding but tick the auto pan box and it really comes to life. Now you'll hear the signal in stereo as it alternates between the left and right speakers. The speed is synced to your song tempo.

Figure 3.48

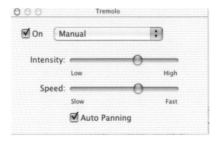

Auto-Wah

Wah-wah was invented to help guitar players imitate the classic talking effect produced by trumpet and trombone players when they use a plunger mute. Of course
guitarists can't use plunger mutes so they use a pedal instead, to open and close
a special filter. In GarageBand the filter is triggered automatically, according to the
intensity of the signal. You can choose from six filters – thick, thin, peak and classic 1-3 – and alter the character of the sound and the intensity of the effect.
Obviously you don't get the fine degree of control available with a foot pedal but
nevertheless, interesting results can be achieved, depending on the source material. Start messing with the presets, to get a general idea how it works.

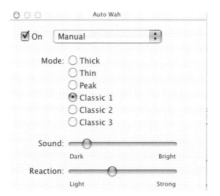

Figure 3.49

Amp simulation

This is the GarageBand effect that gets the most attention, and understandably so,
because you can choose between four classic guitar amplifier emulations – two
British and two American – at the click of a mouse. Use the pre-gain control to
increase your input signal. The further to the right you move the slider, the more
distortion you get. Beneath the pre-gain slider you'll find three tone controls; low,
mid and high. Use the presence control to lift the guitar in a muddy mix. Master
and output controls both control volume.

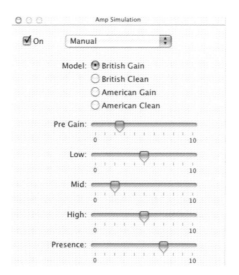

Figure 3.50

That's it as far as GarageBand's insert effects are concerned but of course, you can use any of the Audio Unit effects that come bundled with OS X. They will appear in the insert list, immediately below the GarageBand effects.

Mixing – master effects

Still in the track info window, below the insert effects you'll see two more effects; echo and reverb. These are known as 'send' effects and are not totally track specific. Although you control the amount used on each individual track, using the sliders, the type of reverb or echo effect chosen and their overall settings are determined in the Master Track. And where's that? It's settings are always available from the track info window. Just click the tab labelled Master.

If you're in the main GarageBand user interface, pressing Command-B also reveals GarageBand's Master Track in the track list. Once opened, select it and press Command-I (or double click the track), to access the track info window. Now you can access and edit the reverb and echo parameters.

Figure 3.51

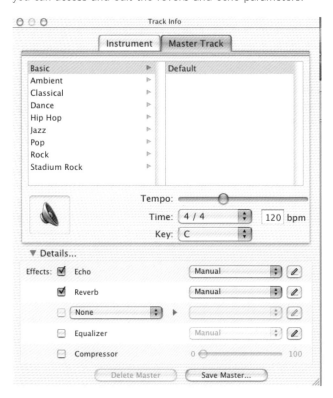

Echo

In essence, this is the same as Track Echo, discussed earlier. So, if you intend applying it to more than one track at a time, making it available globally – here on the master track – will use less of your computer's processing power than inserting on a track-by-track basis. Once you've established your master echo settings, return to the individual tracks to adjust the individual send levels.

Reverb

Last but certainly not least because this is the effect you will probably use the most. And that's the main reason for it being available globally. Reverb is used to simulate the acoustic environment of your music. Use the reverb time parameter to determine the size of your virtual space. The longer the setting, the larger the room. Use the colour slider to control the frequencies.

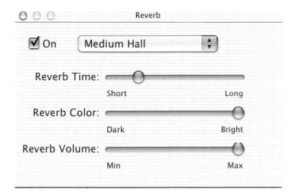

Figure 3.52

GarageBand has a large selection of rooms, halls and even cathedrals to choose from and using them as starting points is usually the best way to go. For example, suppose you've composed and recorded a guitar based rock song. You wouldn't choose a cathedral simulation because rock bands sound awful playing in huge, empty and echoey buildings. It would better to select a medium hall or live stage reset instead and perhaps tweak the parameters slightly. Alter them too much though and you might just as well start again, with a different preset. Where should you place the volume slider? It doesn't really matter if you leave the volume at maximum because you can set independent levels for each track. Once you've established your master reverb settings, return to the individual tracks to adjust the individual send levels.

The Master Track

GarageBand's Master Track is the virtual equivalent of a hardware mixer's master faders. All your individual tracks pass through here before being sent to iTunes as a two-track stereo mixdown. Unlike the instrument tracks it doesn't have a mixer but it does contain a volume curve. In most cases, once you've set your overall master volume you'll probably only use the master track's volume curve to create fade-outs at the end of some types of songs.

You've already discovered that the echo and reverb parameters are determined in the master track info window. However, cast your eyes lower and you'll see another blank insert slot, an equaliser and a compression slider. But EQ and compression facilities are available on the instrument tracks, so what are these for?

You can use these extra effects to add a final touch of gloss to your mix. Just as you might have used compression to add punch to a bass track, you now have the opportunity to do the same across the entire mix. But only, of course, if it needs it.

A number of excellent presets are available. But beware, because most of them will alter your existing reverb and echo settings as well, which is often undesirable.

Using the presets as a starting point and restoring your own reverb and echo settings is a better way to go.

Figure 3.53

Exporting a mix to iTunes

Once you're satisfied with the mix exporting it to iTunes is simplicity itself:

From the file menu select, guess what?…'Export to iTunes'. Before you do so, check the master level meters. Are they clipping (showing red) at any point in the song? If so, reduce your volume in the master track a little or (now here's your chance to use that compressor in the master track) apply a small amount of compression to the mix. You're done. You can now play your song in iTunes along with all pro stuff you've downloaded at the iTunes music store.

Burn a copy to CD (explained later in the book) and play your master on as many different audio systems as possible. If anything needs correcting – maybe it's bass heavy or perhaps lacking in punch – you can return to GarageBand and tweak the mix using the processing tools in the master track's info window.

Where next?

To find out about GarageBand 2's new features read the next chapter. If you're interested in making music on the Apple Mac using applications other than GarageBand read Chapter 5: Beyond GarageBand. If you want to know more about MP3s and iTunes, read Chapter 7: Getting Your Music Out There.

GarageBand 2 – what's new?

All new Macs now ship with iLife 05 which includes GarageBand 2. Here's a rundown of the important new features.

8-track recording

GarageBand 2 now lets you record on nine simultaneous tracks (eight Real Instrument tracks and one Software instrument track), as opposed to just one, in the original version. Of course, to take advantage of this new feature, you will need an audio interface capable of accepting up to eight channels of audio. There's also an extra button, in the track controls, for enabling and disabling recording.

Tune up

A built-in instrument tuner is now available on Real Instrument tracks for guitarists. It works on one note at a time. If you're sharp or flat, the tuner displays red. When you're in tune, it displays green.

Figure 4.1
Instrument tuner.

What's the score?

Many musicians prefer to edit their MIDI data using notation. Music notation is now displayed in the track editor for Software tracks. Basic editing facilities are provided but sadly, none for printing.

Sim amp

New amp simulations are provided for guitar as well as a new Bass Amp simulation.

Correction centre

Perhaps the singer is a little off key. Maybe the bass player has played a note that's not dead on the beat. New advanced recording tools are now provided in the track editor, to fix both timing and tuning.

Figure 4.2

Figure 4.3
Fix timing and tuning

It works like this: GarageBand analyses the waveform patterns and frequencies (for pitch and timing) and determines what the note is supposed to be and where the downbeat is. By using the two sliders you can make corrections. Gentle slider movements are best. Move the sliders into the max and min zones and you'll do more harm than good!

Gender bender

A new effect, Vocal Transformer, is included for pitch-shifting your voice by as much as two octaves up or down. As usual in GarageBand using it is simple. Just move the slider.

Bend it, shape it

In version 1, you could always stretch and pitch shift Apple loops. You can now do this with audio tracks that you record yourself, all the while retaining perfect synchronisation with the rest of your project. For example, you've recorded a guitar part along with an Apple drum loop at 150bpm. You decide to slow things down to 125bpm. The drum loop slows perfectly. In the previous version of GarageBand the guitar track would have continued playing at 150bpm. But in GarageBand 2, the guitar behaves just like the drum loop and slows to 125bpm.

You can also change the key of that guitar part (by single note intervals) but not on the fly. In other words, not during playback. You can also slow down or speed up the track 'and' change the key which is pretty amazing when you think about.

Changing the key of a complete song is also possible. The Master Track now features a pitch curve to add key changes.

Figure 4.4

Lock up

For some inexplicable reason GarageBand is something of a CPU hog (far more so than Logic, believe it or not). However, in version 2 Apple have included a new feature, Locking Tracks, to help improve performance. Locking tracks renders the audio to your Mac's hard disk. Be careful though because locking tracks also eats up large amounts hard disk space very quickly. Tracks can be unlocked and edited in the normal way.

Figure 4.5

Left right, left right...

You could only automate a track's volume in version 1. GarageBand 2 provides automation for track panning as well.

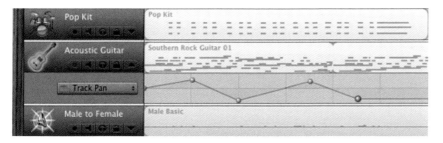

Figure 4.6
Automate track panning

Roll your own

You can now convert a track to an Apple Loop, tag it and add it to your Apple loop library. There's also a new sorting feature. Clicking on the Loops title bar displays specific groups, such as a Jam Pack or another third party collection.

Open MIDI files

You can now import MIDI files into GarageBand 2. Individual instruments are automatically spread across separate tracks.

Musical typing

The on-screen keyboard in the first version of GarageBand is practically unusable, as far as playing goes. However, GarageBand 2 provides an alternative Musical Typing (Shift-Command-K) window to use your computer's keyboard as a make-do piano. Play the white keys using the middle row of keys (a to l) on your keyboard. For sharps and flats, use the top row (w to p).

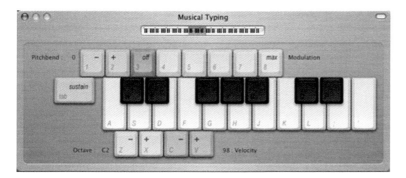

Figure 4.7

Touchy feely

A new Keyboard Sensitivity Slider can be found in the Audio/MIDI tab of GarageBand's preferences. Move the slider to the left and your MIDI keyboard becomes less touch sensitive. The original on-screen keyboard is still there and it's now resizable.

Beyond GarageBand

As brilliant as Garage Band is, any music software that's given away free with a new computer is bound to have some limitations. The big drawback to the original GarageBand was, of course, the lack of true multitrack recording. You could only record on one track at a time. But with GarageBand 2 you can now record on eight tracks in one pass. This makes it an ideal choice for mobile laptop recording at gigs and so on.

Audio editing too has improved in GarageBand 2, with the introduction of limited time-stretching and pitch shifting facilities.

However, despite the improvements, GarageBand remains an entry level program. For truly professional results, full control of your external MIDI gear, topflight sequencing and recording facilities and access to professional audio sampling and editing tools you'll need to look further afield. If you thought GarageBand was powerful, wait until you find out about Logic, Cubase and Digital Performer, three of best known audio software packages available for the Mac.

Logic, Cubase and Digital Performer

If you've bought a new Mac and read the preceding section, by now, you'll be familiar with GarageBand and what you can do with it. In essence, it's a cut-down version of Logic 7, Apple's flagship audio suite. Logic has been around since the dawn of MIDI sequencing and began life on the Atari computer platform as Notator, back in the 80s. Its main rival over the years has been Cubase and to a lesser extent, MOTU's Digital Performer.

All three of these 'super sequencers' are used professionally for studio recording, film scoring, live performance and loop based audio production. In fact most of the music you hear today is created at least in part with one of these programs. In some cases it may be the only music software used.

Logic is the most expensive of the three and since being acquired by the Apple corporation, the most comprehensive. A staggering array of software instruments, an integrated sampler, a convolution reverb, high-end audio processing tools and CD burning software are all included with Logic 7. And of course, Logic, now being under the Apple umbrella, is optimised for the PowerPC G5 processor and Mac OS X.

Although Cubase SX doesn't come bundled with quite as many plug-ins or an integrated sampler it costs considerably less than Logic 7. Steinberg, the company responsible for Cubase, sell their HALion sampler as a VST plug-in. Unlike Logic which uses Core Audio and Audio Unit plug-ins, Cubase uses Steinberg's ASIO

(Audio Stream Input/Output) and VST (Virtual Studio Instrument) technologies respectively. Although you can't use Audio Units with Cubase most third party developers provide support for VST alongside AU.

In contrast to Logic and Cubase, Digital Performer has always been a Mac only product and now provides full support for OS X Core Audio and Core MIDI. And although DP comes bundled with a set of MAS plug-ins (MOTU's own format) it fully supports the Audio Unit format. That means you can take full advantage of the growing number of AU freeware plug-ins floating around on the Web as well as those included with OS X.

Just like GarageBand, these sequencers have a main user interface, with the tracks displayed vertically and the recorded MIDI data and audio events shown as blocks – called regions or parts – on a horizontal timeline. And just as GarageBand has tape recorder style transport controls, so too do Logic, Cubase and Digital Performer.

Now you may think that because these programs appear to have extra features dotted about the main GUI – such as track parameter views, mixing controls and intriguing looking toolsets – on the face of it, they look remarkably similar to GarageBand. So what's the big deal?

Figure 5.1
Logic's Arrange page

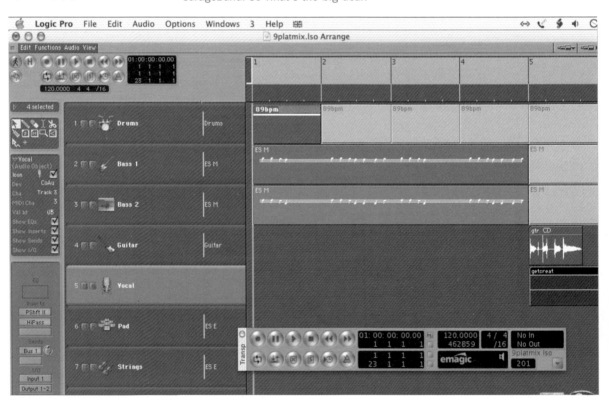

On the surface, yes, they do look much the same but it's a very different story behind the scenes. Let's take a look some of the many features included with these grown-up sequencers and discover what you can beyond GarageBand.

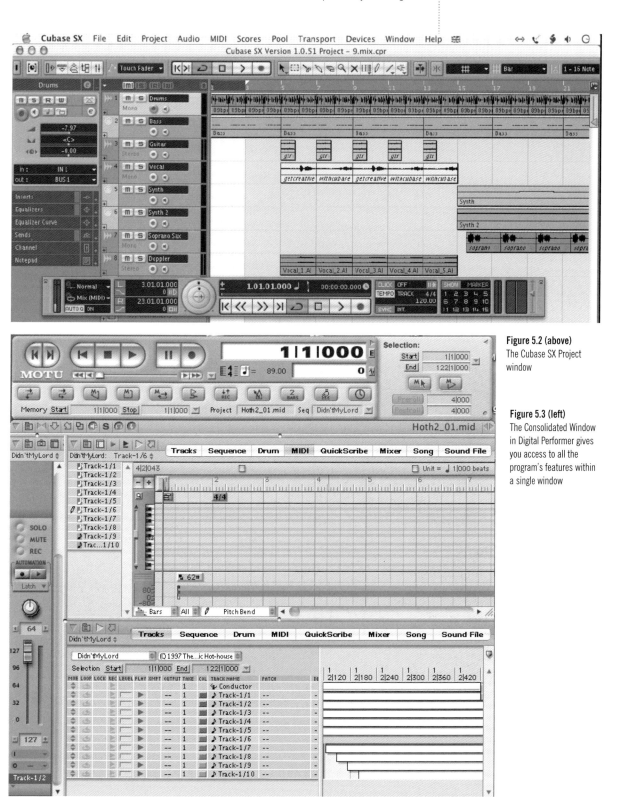

Figure 5.2 (above)
The Cubase SX Project
window

Figure 5.3 (left)
The Consolidated Window
in Digital Performer gives
you access to all the
program's features within
a single window

Make time and tempo changes

Beginning a new project in Logic and Cubase is similar to GarageBand with a default tempo of 120 bpm and a time signature of 4/4 (the most commonly used settings for modern popular music). However, unlike with GarageBand, you don't specify a key signature. The underlying reason for doing so in GarageBand being that it functions mainly as a loop production tool. Apple Loops are tagged with a key signature.

If you're writing and recording music that requires a change of tempo at some point you can't do it in GarageBand. Neither can you insert a new time signature in a song; not if you're using the metronome anyway. However, using a full-fledged sequencer will provide you with full control over all aspects of time and tempo. You'll be able to insert as many time and signature changes as you need into your compositions. Changes of tempo can be recorded on-the-fly or drawn and edited in a special tempo track.

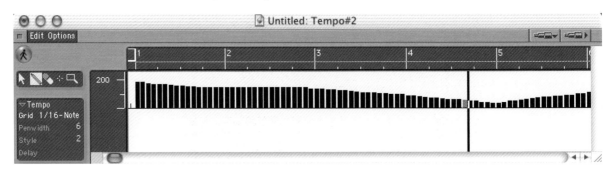

Figure 5.4
Above: Logic's Tempo Graphic Editor. Below:
The Tempo Track in Cubase SX

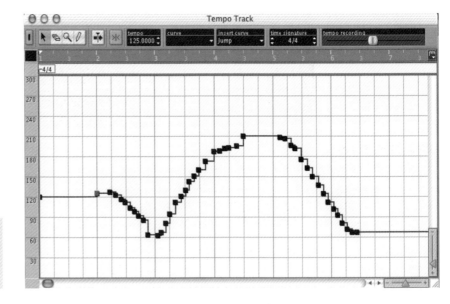

Info

Time signature events can only be positioned at the beginning of bars. Think about it.

Tip

When recording freely, without a sequencer clock, musicians will wander a few bpm either side of the tempo throughout a song. If you're recording a sequence that emulates a real performance, enter a sprinkling of tempo changes in your sequencer's tempo track. This will help the music breathe a little

A glance at the track list in Logic or Cubase reveals a type not found in GarageBand; a plain old fashioned MIDI track. What are they for, you might be thinking? Well, they're incredibly useful, especially for controlling any hardware synthesisers or sound modules you happen to own.

Pre-recorded MIDI data can also be used to control many other kinds of external equipment; stage lighting being a perfect example. Many performers now use a PowerBook and Logic to control their on-stage backing tracks and also their lighting rigs, using MIDI tracks.

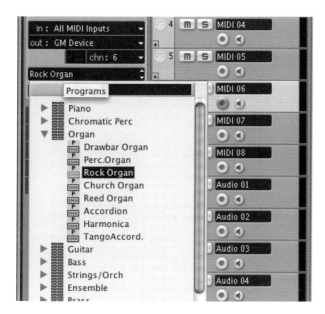

Figure 5.5
A Cubase SX MIDI track being used to control a General MIDI sound module

Make your own loops

Logic supports Apple Loops, which behave just as they do in GarageBand; expanding and contracting to fit the song tempo. Cubase and Digital Performer support REX files (incidentally, so does Logic) which are much the same thing.

You can make your own Apple Loops in Logic using the Apple Loops Utility (you can also do this in GarageBand 2). It detects and marks the transients of an audio file. These markers provide a reference for Logic, allowing realtime stretching of the audio data. You can also tag them with data which makes them easy to find in Logic's loop browser.

Apple Loops may be a buzz word at the moment but Propellerhead Software began the slicing and dicing craze with their ReCycle software which produces REX files. Both Cubase and Digital Performer support REX files and provide tools for slic-

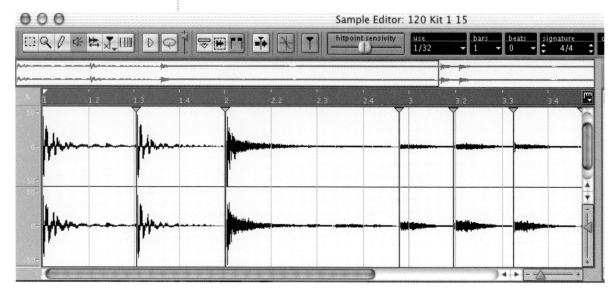

Figure 5.6
Audio transients detected using Hitpoints in Cubase SX

ing audio and producing loops that will adjust to any given tempo, just like Apple Loops.

24-bit recording

The major sequencing packages provide recording resolutions up to 32-bit and sample rates of 44.1, 48, 88.2 and 96kHz. Providing that you record them properly, this yields superior quality audio files compared to those recorded in GarageBand which only supports 16-bit recording.

Although you can get the job done, compared to Logic, Cubase and Digital Performer, GarageBand's recording facilities are pretty crude. Tasks like auto-drop recording (for repairing mistakes), merge recording (useful for layering MIDI drum tracks), cycle recording, setting up count-ins are either impossible in GarageBand or awkward to implement. Not only are these commonplace recording operations rendered quick and easy in a pro sequencer you'll also find many sophisticated and very useful options like toggling between play and record and retrospective recording (capture a fantastic take even though you forgot to press record).

Record on multiple tracks

GarageBand 2 now provides eight-track simultaneous recording but only on audio tracks (real instrument tracks). Logic, Cubase and Digital Performer allow simultaneous recording on both audio and MIDI tracks. You can also record sophisticated continuous MIDI data such as program changes and system exclusive messages (useful for controlling your external synths and sound modules).

Extensive and detailed editing

In GarageBand you have a single track editor which, let's face it, is a bit on the small side and fairly limited in scope. Splash out and buy a full-fledged audio pack-

Info

If your Mac or audio hardware only has 16-bit inputs there's nothing to be gained by selecting 24-bit recording in your sequencer – except larger files with exactly the same audio quality.

Info

System Exclusive data is recorded on a MIDI track and used to control a specific hardware device. Each manufacturer – Roland, Korg, Yamaha and so on – has a unique set of Sysex messages.

age though and you'll never return to GarageBand, at least not for editing. Apart from the numerous menu selectable editing facilities available in the main GUIs of Logic, Cubase and Digital Performer, it's the sheer scope of audio and MIDI manipulation available, behind the scenes, in the dedicated editors, that makes these programs so powerful.

All three programs provide a classic 'piano roll' grid editor for editing MIDI. Logic has a Matrix editor, SX has a Key Editor and Digital Performer has a MIDI Graphic editor. The principle is the same as the track editor in GarageBand with notes displayed on a grid with their pitch referenced to a virtual keyboard. You can perform precise graphical editing in these editors – on several tracks at once, if necessary – such as fine-tuning the velocities, positions and lengths of notes. You can also add notes to the grid using a pencil tool.

Figure 5.7
Logic's Matrix editor – note the tool set, to the left of the keyboard

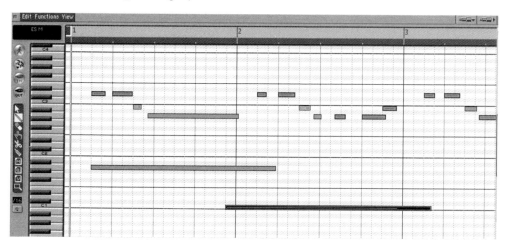

You can't enter notes and beats into GarageBand but Logic, Cubase and Digital Performer provide facilities to do this in almost all their track editors. All three programs have a grid editor dedicated to drums where you can add beats to the timeline and program your own rhythm parts, drum machine style.

Figure 5.8
The Drum Editor in Cubase SX

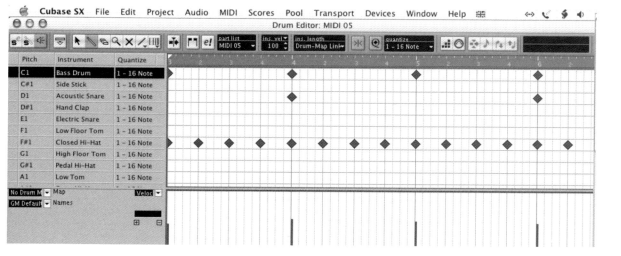

Figure 5.9
Logic's List Editor

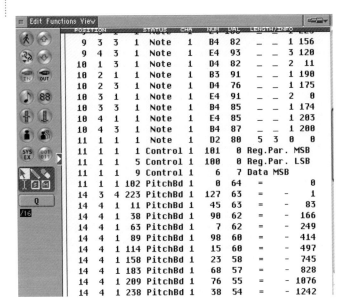

Figure 5.10
The Score Editor in Cubase SX

When it comes to recording and fine tuning controller info GarageBand doesn't have much to offer. But sometimes a detailed numerical representation of MIDI data is absolutely necessary, particularly when setting up and editing data sent to your external synthesisers and sound modules. The grown-up sequencer packages of this world offer list based editing, for those who need it.

Instead of using the graphical editors, many musicians and students prefer to work in the score editors provided in Logic, Cubase and Digital Performer. You can either enter notes directly onto the scores or play them in and edit them afterwards. You can also prepare scores, extract instrument parts and print everything out. GarageBand 2 does allow limited notation editing but you can't enter notes directly onto the score. Neither can you print out scores and instrument parts.

Audio editing in the original GarageBand was practically non-existent. All you could do was cut, paste and move audio regions in a song. In GarageBand 2, things have improved considerably with the addition of pitch transposition and time compression and expansion. But for getting your hands dirty and delving deeper into the black arts of creative audio editing, there are many more tools available in the major audio suites. For example, using Logic's sample editor you can process individual audio files in ways not possible in GarageBand such as:

• Normalise an audio file. In other words, raise the volume level of an audio signal to its highest possible level, without introducing distortion.
• Raise or lower the gain of a passage of audio.
• Create fade-ins and fade-outs in an audio file.
• Reverse the phase of selected audio material (in other words, it will sound back-to-front).
• Remove undesirable direct current (DC) which is sometimes layered over audio signals causing a vertical shift in the waveform.
• Search for peaks in the waveform and for momentary sections of silence.

Figure 5.11
Time Machine, Silencer and Audio Energizer,
just three of Logic's eight audio Factory tools

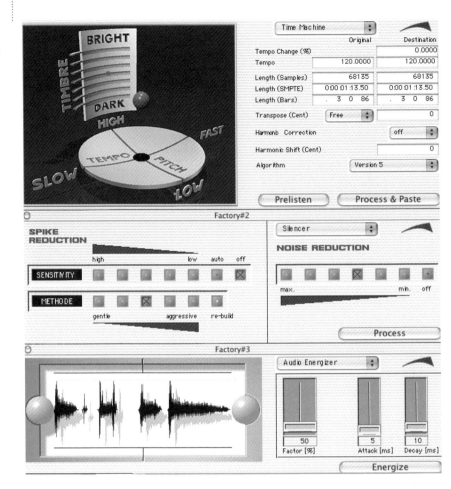

Logic's audio Factory also provides a creative set of sophisticated time compression/expansion and transposition tools which are far superior to anything found in GarageBand. Cubase and Digital Performer provide similar functions and tools.

Virtual mixing consoles

GarageBand's simple mixing facilities are easy to use but if you're serious about recording, before long you'll be looking for ways to control and fine tune your mix in ways that GarageBand just isn't designed to do. Logic, Cubase and Digital Performer have sophisticated mixers modelled on conventional hardware recording consoles with channel strips and faders. Plug-ins such as dynamic signal processors, reverbs and so on can be placed in the audio signal path using the same inserts and auxiliary sends commonly found on their hardware counterparts.

Automation too is far more comprehensive in these programs. Not only can you automate track volume and pan, you can also draw detailed parameter adjustments to any plug-ins inserted on a channel such as reverb density, compressor settings

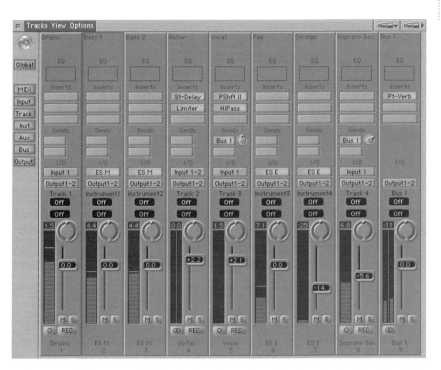

Figure 5.12
Logic's Adaptive Track Mixer

and so on. Of course, all the track automation data is reflected in the mixer. Likewise, anything you record as automation data when using the virtual mixing consoles is reflected in the track automation.

Figure 5.13
Automation data, seen here in Logic's Arrange page

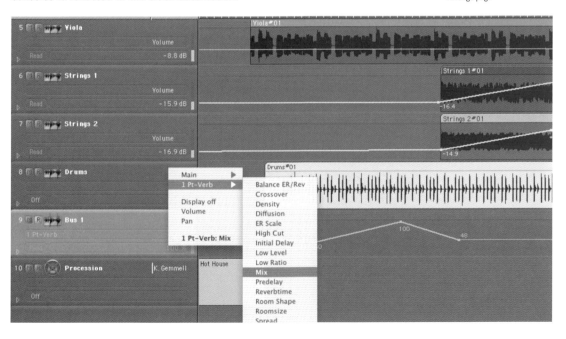

Full-featured dynamics processors and effects units

GarageBand's dynamics processors and effects plug-ins are mostly trimmed down versions of those found in Logic 7 with fewer parameters and simplified controls. But the dynamics and effects processors included with Cubase, Logic and Digital Performer offer more controls and features with attractive GUI's, modelled on their hardware equivalents.

On page 52 we discussed how a compressor can be used to tighten up the dynamics of a signal by reducing the difference in levels between loud and soft passages. In GarageBand you simply apply compression using a slider. But Logic's Compressor, for example, looks and behaves like a typical analogue compressor. It works like this:

Firstly, using a slider, you set a threshold level for the incoming audio signal. This is measured in decibels (dB). When the signal exceeds this level, the compressor attenuates it by a value that you set with a ratio slider. A ratio of 6:1, for example, will reduce an incoming signal that lies 6 dB above the threshold, by 1 dB. Now everything below the threshold level remains the same but the louder signals are reduced.

Now because the compressor has lowered the input signal level, the volume of its output signal is probably lower and needs to be increased. You can do this with a gain slider. It's easier though to let the compressor's auto gain feature handle this for you (not all compressors have this feature but Logic's Compressor does).

Compressors typically have attack and release controls. You use the attack control to determine how quickly the compressor reacts to signals above the threshold level. High settings ensure that the original attack of a sound (a plucked guitar string for example) is allowed through. You use the release control to determine how long it takes the compressor to stop dampening the signal, once it falls below the threshold level.

This kind of compression (where the compressor kicks in immediately above a predetermined threshold level) is referred to by audio engineers as a 'hard knee' type. But for smoother results you use the knee slider to gradually apply the compression, before and after the threshold level (soft knee compression).

Apart from the extra controls found on high-end dynamics plug-ins, they usually include useful visual indicators of what's actually happening. For example, Logic's Compressor features a gain reduction meter (to show you how much compression is actually taking place) and a graphical display depicting the threshold levels and compression ratios used.

Figure 5.14
Logic's Compressor has all the controls found on a typical analogue compressor

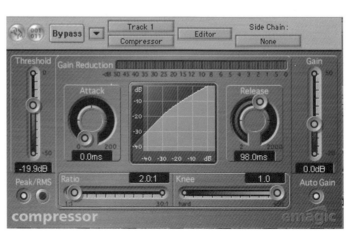

GarageBand provides EQ facilities for cutting and boosting treble, mid and bass frequencies. But only the mid frequency band is adjustable. However, both Logic and Digital Performer feature an eight-band parametric EQ plug-in with a graphical editing display. Cubase has a four-band parametric EQ, also with a graphical display. These types of plug-ins allow you to set and adjust the frequency band parameters either directly in the graphical display or with more conventional controls such as virtual knobs. For many people, this is a much more intuitive method of working than just using the sliders provided in GarageBand.

As you've probably discovered, you can control three reverb parameters in GarageBand: time, colour and volume. But reverb is a vital part of audio production and as your your mixing expertise develops you'll be looking for more control. Using Logic's GoldVerb, for example, you can control the early reflections of a simulated acoustic space including pre-delay, room size, room shape and even the virtual placement of two microphones. Once you've created your room, a hall or even a cathedral you can then fine tune the delays, the diffusion of the reverb tail and the amount of time it takes the reverb to die away. You can even simulate the surface of the walls (glass, stone, wood panelling and so on) using a high cut filter.

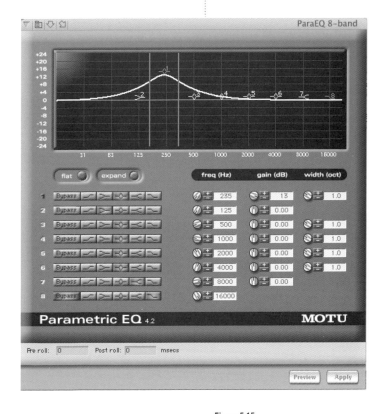

Figure 5.15
Digital Performer's 8-band Parametric EQ. You can adjust EQ settings by dragging directly on the EQ graph

Figure 5.16
Logic's GoldVerb reverb plug-in

Synchronisation facilities

GarageBand doesn't provide any means to synchronise your projects to external equipment. And why should you want to do that? Well to be frank, if you're sketching out a project or recording a demo in GarageBand you probably wouldn't need to hook up to any external hardware anyway. But once you're involved in audio production at a more professional level you may well need to synchronise your computer generated MIDI tracks with an external audio recorder or maybe a video deck. To do that your sequencer must be synchronised to run at exactly the same time and tempo as your hardware devices. Logic, Cubase and Digital Performer are capable of receiving and transmitting the complete range of professional synchronisation protocols.

Figure 5.17
Logic's synchronisation window

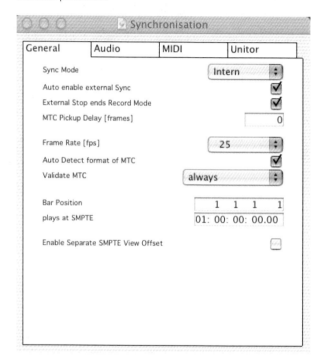

Sound to picture

Do you harbour ambitions to compose for film and television? Perhaps you're interested in adding soundtracks to your home movies. Logic, Cubase and Digital Performer provide all the facilities you need. All three programs allow you to import QuickTime movies and synchronise playback with both MIDI and audio tracks. This is an extremely powerful feature and far more convenient than the old fashioned method of hooking up to a video deck. Without the trials and tribulations of slaving to external time code you can instantly locate any spot in the movie, advance back and forth one frame at a time and even set up loops.

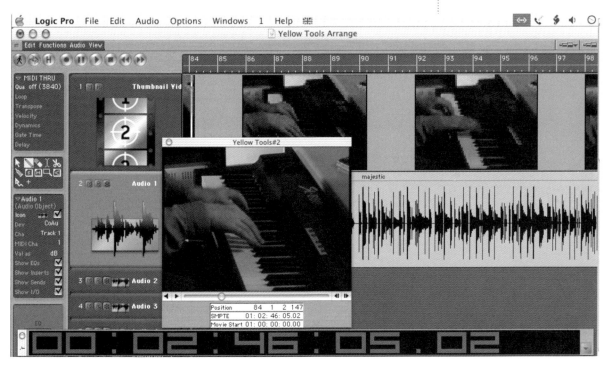

Figure 5.18
Synchronised video and audio tracks in Logic Pro

Samplers

Although samplers began life as hardware devices these days they've been mostly replaced by their software equivalents. But what exactly is a sampler?

At its simplest, a sampler plays pre-recorded sounds. These may be an integral part of the software, supplied on a CD/DVD or maybe downloaded off the Web.

A true sampler enables you to capture sounds and map them to different key ranges across a virtual piano keyboard. They're usually triggered and played back by a MIDI keyboard. You can also use them to record entire musical phrases which can be replayed at the touch of a key.

However, the trend today is towards plug-in sample players that run as virtual instruments within a host sequencer, just like the software instruments included with GarageBand. Many of these have their own built-in sound sets as well as providing facilities to import standard audio files and convert samples from other formats.

Of course, GarageBand is perfectly capable of running a software sampler but it's arguable, that beyond the freeware plug-ins like iDrum, purchasing a full-fledged sampler might just be considered overkill for use with an entry level sequencer.

Logic ships with a built-in sampler, the EXS24. It's a very powerful and flexible piece of software in its own right, providing all the facilities found in a hardware sampler. You can import samples, to build your own instruments or use the bundled factory set.

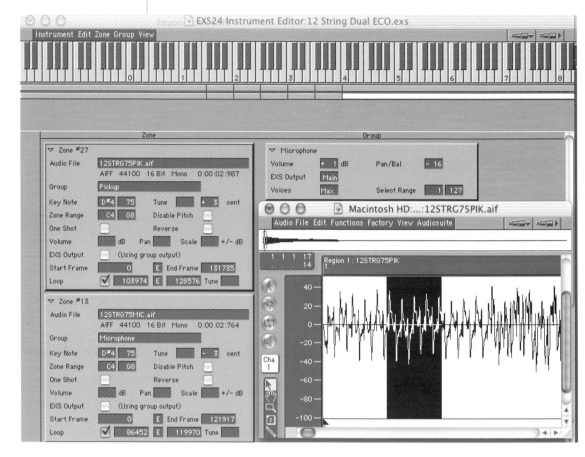

Figure 5.19
Two windows are
used to operate
Logic's EXS24
sampler: The
Instrument Editor
window (top), where
you organise your
samples and map
them to key ranges
(you also have direct
access to Logic's
sample editor from
here);
The plug-in window
(bottom), where you
edit parameters such
as filter and envelope
settings

The EXS24 only runs within Logic. No other sequencers are supported. But the makers of Cubase (Steinberg) and Digital Performer (MOTU) both manufacture soft-samplers (HALion and Mach Five respectively) that can be used in all three of the major sequencing packages.

Sample libraries

All three of the samplers mentioned above come with their own libraries which may be all you need. However, these are usually a mixed bag of instruments and loops designed to appeal across a broad musical spectrum. Most musicians and producers, after first getting to grips with their sampler, inevitably, begin looking further afield for specific musical material to suit their needs

For professional composers, there are some absolutely massive sample libraries available. The Vienna Symphonic Library, for example, weighs in at nearly 240 GB, comes on 16 DVDs and costs in the region of £3000. Although far less costly, some of the upmarket drum libraries are almost as large. Fxpansion's BFG (Big Friendly Drummer) is supplied on 10 DVDs.

An increasing trend among sample library producers is the inclusion of a 'front end' with their products (commonly Native Instrument's Kompakt Player). In other words, what you get is a set of samples bundled with a convenient and easy-to-use player. From the users perspective, the main advantage of using this type of product (commonly referred to as a ROMpler) is that the tedious work of key and velocity mapping has been done for you. The main disadvantage is that usually, you can't import other sample formats. Neither can you perform any waveform editing.

A similar trend is the emergence of sample-based virtual instruments from sound designers. For example Yellow Tools now produce sample based MVI's (Modular Virtual Instruments) in addition to their sample libraries. Their bass instrument, Majestic, comes with a 4 DVD set of sampled bass guitars and a 100 year old double bass.

Figure 5.20
Majestic, an incredibly realistic bass instrument from Yellow Tools, is one of the new breed of sample based virtual instruments

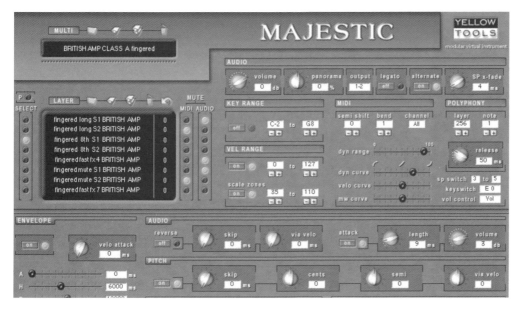

Figure 5.21

IK Multimedia's virtual workstation, SampleTank 2, contains a huge collection of instrument samples

Another example of the all-in-one approach to sample players is SampleTank2 a complete virtual workstation. If your music is fairly conventional in nature, SampleTank 2 is probably all you need by way of a sound module. And apart from a generous sound set of its own, you can also import other sample formats.

SampleTank 2's sister program, Sonic Synth also contains an extensive library of sounds. But unlike SampleTank 2, which in the main contains samples of conventional instruments, SonicSynth 2 is crammed with samples from a huge range of classic analogue synthesisers. In fact, with both programs on your hard drive you can probably produce just about any style of music imaginable.

Score writing and self-publishing

In the not very distant past, composers and arrangers used to write their scores by hand. And although there is no denying that a handsomely hand-written manuscript is a sight to behold, more often than not the end result looked as if the composer's dog had written the music. The difficult task of deci-phering the scribble and preparing readable instrumental parts was left to the unfortunate music copyist. But that's all changed because, in most cases, profes-sional composers and arrangers now use computer software to write their music. And more often than not, they work with a MIDI keyboard and a score package such as Sibelius or a MIDI sequencer like Logic.

The main advantages of using computer software to write and print music, as opposed to writing it by hand, are obvious. The results are easy to read, mistakes are easily corrected (sometimes automatically) and you can play back the score. You can also print as many copies as you like without using a photo copying serv-ice. So how do you get started with notation software on the Mac?

Free notes

Although GarageBand 2 includes a basic notation editor, you can't print the music displayed on the screen. Apple will have you believe that using GarageBand's nota-tion editor is a great way to learn how to read and write music. But to be frank, that's not really true. Admittedly, you do see notes on the screen, when you play one of the software instruments, but you can't enter notes on the stave – you can only move them around.

If you're new to music notation software, rather than struggle with the notation in GarageBand, a far better way to get started is to download a copy of NotePad (www.finalemusic.com/notepad). This is a cut down version of Finale with an amaz-ing amount of features considering it's free. You're allowed to create scores with up to eight staves, in any key and with any common time signature. You can enter notes and rests down to a value of a 32nd note, add slurs, dynamic markings and all the common articulations. In fact it's such a good program there is even a book about it (Finale NotePad Primer). Of course, being a free program, it has its limi-tations but nothing that will concern the beginner.

Figure 6.1
Easy music (top) and difficult music
(bottom) scored with NotePad, Finale's free
score program

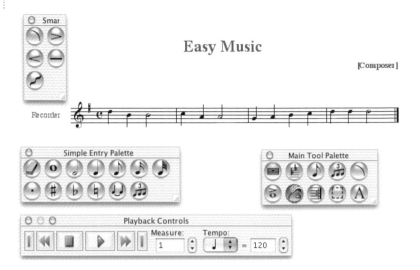

Another too-good-to-be-true feature with NotePad is its ability to import any score prepared with another program in the Finale family. And that includes downloading files from the Finale Showcase, a place where composers, arrangers, educators and students post their work. Anyone can browse the showcase and view downloaded files here for free.

The Finale ladder

PrintMusic

Although NotePad provides playback facilities, once you've mastered the basics of music notation you'll probably want to print out your music and hear it played by real musicians. But there is an obstacle. You can't extract and print out the individual instrument parts (although you can print the entire score). To do that you'll have to upgrade to PrintMusic, a true entry level notation package that's also suitable for undemanding professional work. With PrintMusic you can create scores with up to 24 staves, create lead sheets with lyrics, chord symbols and guitar fretboards. You can also scan sheet music for transposing or rearranging. But most importantly, you can extract and print out the instrumental parts.

Allegro

The next step on the Finale ladder is Allegro, a full-featured notation package ideally suited to professional musicians, educators and students. Apart from a very comprehensive set of score writing tools you can also save your work as audio files.

Finale

The top rung of the ladder is occupied by Finale itself which does just about anything you could possibly ask of a notation package. Like Sibelius (we'll get to that soon) it's used by symphonic, jazz and film composers. In the US it's a popular program with schools and colleges (it's half the price of Sibelius) but it hasn't really caught on in a big way with the British educational establishment. Although the problem has been rectified, for a long time Finale was considered a difficult-to-use application. In the UK this reputation has been hard to shake off, particularly with the stiff competition coming from the Sibelius camp, Finale's main rival.

Sibelius v Finale

In the mid to late 90s Finale were the undisputed leaders of the field in the notation software stakes. You could say it was a one horse race. However, although capable of producing superb sheet music, some musicians found the program complex and difficult to use.

Finale remained unchallenged until Sibelius joined the running. Both programs were similar in many respects but Sibelius boasted an 'easy to use' interface and moved quickly from the back of the field to challenge the front runner. Naturally enough, Finale quickened its pace and the race has been neck and neck ever since.

Improving and updating these programs (in the case of Finale, on an annual basis) must present a challenge to their programmers. After all, they already produce first class sheet music. The accent then, must be on improving the ease of use and general musicality of the programs. To do that means understanding exactly who is likely to use notation software and why. Sibelius Software and Make Music, (the company responsible for Finale) certainly know their markets and in contrast with the major sequencing manufacturers, aim their products fair and square at three distinct types of users – teachers and students; music publishers; composers and arrangers. They do it brilliantly, hitting the target perfectly with all three.

Both Finale 2005 and Sibelius 3 come with substantial printed manuals. They're

Info

A new feature to Sibelius 3, Flexitime, understands when you're playing rubato style (in and out of tempo) when recording music into the program. You don't need to set a quantize value - Sibelius does it automatically and displays the notes correctly on the staff. Not only that - playback is unaffected.

well written, in a very accessible style and explain everything you need to know about the programs in great detail.

A blank manuscript

You can begin new scores from scratch in Finale and Sibelius with an easy-to-use dialogue for selecting instruments and defining key and time signatures. Alternatively, you can use one of the many score templates which cover a wide style of music. Sibelius even has a special film score template, complete with a time code display above the top staff, devised by the guy who wrote the Simpsons sound-track. These blank manuscripts are the equivalent of the old fashioned printed type which are fast disappearing.

Keeping tabs

Guitarists are also well catered for in both programs. Tab input is easy to use and in Sibelius, you can load and save the popular ASCII tab file format, making it easy to share music with other guitarists via the Internet. Sibelius also includes tab and guitar frames scanning facilities. Both programs include comprehensive sets of fretted instruments.

Figure 6.2
Guitar tab in Sibelius 3

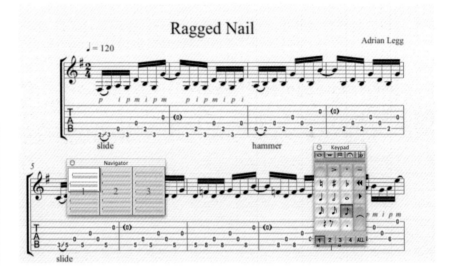

Info

If you play a woodwind or brass instrument you can input notes directly into Finale using a microphone. The technology isn't completely flawless but does a pretty accurate job with uncomplicated music. Of course, you have to play in tune, and in time, for it to work properly!

Skool stuff

Finale and Sibelius are both teacher friendly. For example, if you're a teacher you can disable unnecessary, complicated features in Sibelius, leaving just those need-ed for your student's coursework. Students can't cheat either, in the transposition exercises, by getting Sibelius to transpose parts automatically. You can turn that off too. The program also contains an impressive set of scales and arpeggios. Just about every kind is available, including the more exotic eastern varieties.

And never again will your students play music at double forte in the quiet pas-sages with the usual excuse about not spotting the dynamic markings. You can highlight the quiet bits in red (or whatever colour you like) with Sibelius. Well that's the theory anyway! Seriously though, you can now change the colour of almost anything in the score – notes, text, lines, symbols and so on. They all print in colour too.

Also useful for teachers is the Finale SmartMusic accompaniment system. Basically, it's a practice system for string, brass and woodwind players. It's sold separately but the facility to save scores as SmartMusic accompaniments is built into Finale. This is a great feature enabling you to save files that display a part for the soloist to read as they play along.

But perhaps the most significant educational feature in Finale is the Performance Assessment Wizard. If you're a music teacher this is a real winner because you can use it to prepare simple tunes and exercises for your students to practise. The budding instrumentalists can then play your files using the Finale Performance Assessment application (FPA), practise the music, record it and then assess their performance.

The FPA itself is a clever little player which displays your file as scrolling sheet music. Students can adjust the tempo of the music to suit their playing level. Of course, for instruments other than a MIDI keyboard, they'll need a microphone. When they're satisfied with their performance, they can record it. Now for the clever part. The FPA not only records an audio file, for aural assessment, it also displays the recorded notes on the stave – correctly played notes as green and wrongly played notes as red. Your students can now save their work to disc or maybe e-mail it to you as an MP3.

It's a great idea and works well but you are limited to creating simple one voice files without repeats, multi-rests and note values smaller than 16ths. Even so, it's an excellent practice tool for brass and wind players up to around grade 5 level.

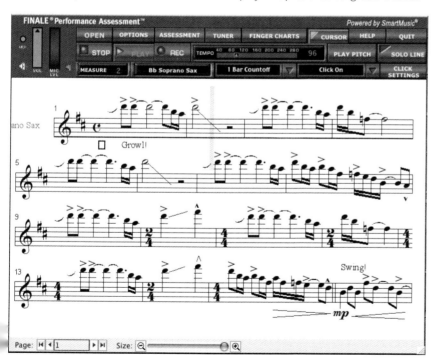

Figure 6.3
The Finale Performance Assessment Player

Info

Anybody who's struggled to get triplets displaying properly with notation software will be overjoyed with the news that Finale 2005 now makes the job easier. Engraver Tuplets is feature that automatically repositions triplets when notes are raised or lowered on the staff. No more crowded notes and collisions.

Time savers

Creating scripts is great time-saver and facilities for doing this can be found in Finale. An example – you have a score for piano and voice and you need to convert the vocal to B flat saxophone. It's easily achieved by creating a script that selects the top staff, replaces 'Voice' with 'Sax', handles the transposition, strips out the lyrics, removes the chord symbols and updates the layout – all in one fell swoop.

Drum grooves

Writing drum parts using conventional notation can be a tricky business – getting the sounds in your head across to a drummer and so on. Of course you can write a simple instruction for the drummer like 'play 16 bars of laid back rock'. In fact many writers do exactly that. However, both Finale and Sibelius provide the option to select a Drum Groove such as Heavy Funk and generate a drum map. Apart from the bundled templates you can add your own MIDI drum grooves and add them to the menu.

A useful Kontakt

Until recently, playing back scores in notation packages was a pretty miserable experience unless you owned a decent sound module. However, Sibelius Software have recently teamed up with Native Instruments to produce Kontakt Player Silver (which ships with Sibelius 3) and Kontakt Player Gold (an extra). The latter adds high-quality playback using 64 pitched and 100 unpitched percussion sounds. They cover the full range needed for composing conventional scores such orchestral music, wind band, jazz ensembles and so on. And they go well beyond the usual GM set too, incorporating instruments such as bass clarinet, baritone horns, and special string techniques. Male and female voices and choirs are also included.

It has to be said, the Kontakt Player's sounds are very good and no doubt broaden the appeal of Sibelius considerably but only 20 are included with the Silver version and only eight can be used in a score. For many users that's not going to be anywhere near sufficient and that means upgrading to Kontakt Player Gold. This is in stark contrast to Finale which includes a similar sample player built into their program.

The human touch

Of course, a big advantage of using the Kontact Player is the ability to save your scores as digital audio files, ready for CD burning and MP3 conversion. You can do this in both programs.

Music entered onto a score with a mouse or via computer keyboard is always going to sound a touch robotic. However, to compensate, both programs feature human playback facilities. These will interpret a score's markings, articulations, dynamics and so on and generate playback that simulates a live performance. Even text markings such as 'rit' or 'cresc' and dynamic markings are recognised.

Figure 6.4
Native Instrument's Kontakt Player provides the sampled sounds for Sibelius

Both programs provide a wide choice of playback styles in the classical, jazz and rock genres along with the option to customise your own. However, although the human playback features in Finale and Sibelius serve as an excellent compositional reference the results can still be less than convincing if you intend recording a demo of your score. In general, notation packages are no substitute for a high end sequencer such as Logic or Cubase when it comes recording and editing MIDI data.

It's a scorcher

You can publish your finished scores via the Internet using Sibelius' amazing Scorch technology. You can do it on your own site or on SibeliusMusic.com, for free. If you want, Sibelius Music will sell your music on your behalf. The deal's a 50-50 split.

Once they've downloaded and installed the free Scorch plug-in on their computer, visitors to your site can play, transpose and even print scores (providing you let them, of course). The technology has been in use for a while now and several major publishers like www.sheetmusicdirect.com are already using it to deliver sheet music commercially.

You first have to save your score in Sibelius, as a Scorch web page, and give it a file name. Sibelius saves two files: an HTML file and a Sibelius score file (with the extension .sib). Both files are sent, via FTP, to your web host.

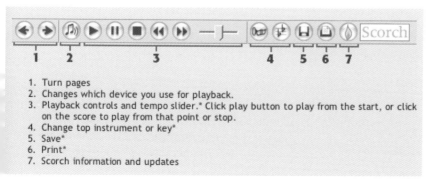

Figure 6.5
Scorch is free software which enables you to view, play, customize and print Sibelius scores on the Internet

1. Turn pages
2. Changes which device you use for playback.
3. Playback controls and tempo slider.* Click play button to play from the start, or click on the score to play from that point or stop.
4. Change top instrument or key*
5. Save*
6. Print*
7. Scorch information and updates

Scoring with Logic, Cubase and Digital Performer

Dedicated notation software such as Finale and Sibelius is expensive. So, assuming you've moved beyond GarageBand, can you prepare professional looking scores and parts using your sequencer? The answer is yes. But it will take you longer.

Sequencers are fantastic tools for recording MIDI data. They also provide a range of facilities for editing the recorded results, including score editors. Generally speaking, provided you're prepared to spend the time, you can produce excellent scores with all three sequencer packages. But do bear in mind that beginning a new score from scratch and entering notes directly onto the stave is slow and cumbersome compared to doing it with a dedicated notation program.

Figure 6.6
Logic provides a comprehensive note and symbol palette

Getting your music out there

One of the best things about making music on the Mac is the immediate contact with the outside world. Write and record a song in GarageBand, save it to iTunes and putting it on the Internet is just a few steps away.

Tag it

Chapter 3 concluded with the simple task of exporting a finished GarageBand song to iTunes, as an audio file. But iTunes has a mind of its own and uses a tagging system to organise and store your songs. So, to prevent you from losing your song, it's a good idea to tag it before you export it. Open GarageBand's preferences and click on the Export icon. Create a new playlist (or use an existing one) and enter the composer's name and the title of your album.

Figure 7.1

Export	

General   Audio/MIDI   Export   Advanced

Song and Playlist Information
GarageBand will use this as the default information when exporting your songs.

iTunes Playlist: PC Publishing Playlist

Composer Name: Keith Gemmell

Album Name: Making Music on the Apple Mac

In the screenshot above, a GarageBand song entitled My Song is exported to a playlist called PC Publishing. The composer is Keith Gemmell and the album is called Making Music on the Apple Mac. The file appeared on the Mac's hard drive under Home > Music > iTunes > iTunes Music > Keith Gemmell > Making Music on the Apple Mac > My Song.aif.

The song appeared in iTunes (below) with the tagged information displayed beneath the relevant headings. Note that iTunes has duplicated the Composer tag as the Artist tag. These can be changed.

Figure 7.2

The tags we applied in GarageBand are fine for organising songs on your hard drive. However, if you intend distributing it over the Internet, it's a good idea to include as much information within the file as possible. So, in iTunes, select your song (or songs) and press Command-I, to open the Song Information dialogue. The Summary page is displayed by default. Open the Info page and add appropriate information about your song.

> ### Info
>
> If you want to know where a song that appears in iTunes is stored on your hard drive, press Control and click on the song. Choose Show Song File from the list of options.

Encode it

GarageBand exports your songs as audio files, in AIFF format. Generally speaking audio files are much too large for Internet distribution. Before uploading them to the Web, you'll need to convert them to MP3 files. MP3 files are compressed, to make them smaller and faster to play and download via the Internet.

There are many utilities for converting AIFF files into MP3 files. But iTunes does the job as well as most of them. However before you begin:

1 Open the iTunes preferences and click on the Importing icon.
2 From the Import Using pop-up menu, select MP3 Encoder.
3 From the Setting pop-up menu choose a quality setting. All three – Good Quality (128 kbps), High Quality (160 kbps) and Higher Quality (192 kbps) – will provide good results but bear in mind that the higher the quality, the larger the file.

The three presets mentioned above will almost always deliver good MP3s but if you prefer more control, select the Custom setting. You have a wider choice of bit-rates here to choose from. For music (speech is OK) don't go below 128kbps. Of course, selecting a higher bit-rate is fine but keep in mind that larger settings result in larger files.

Choosing VBR, as opposed to CBR uses less space and yields better quality audio. However, some older MP3 players will not be able to play files created with the VBR option.

Don't mess with the sample rates (unless you have a good reason) and unless you specifically require a mono recording leave both the Sample and Channel settings at Auto. Always choose the Normal stereo setting, unless you have good reasons for selecting Joint Stereo.

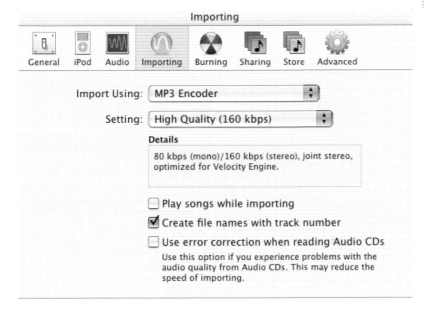

Figure 7.3

Leave the Smart Encoder (iTunes overrides any daft settings you may have made) and the Filter Frequencies below 10Hz ticked (frequencies this low can't be heard by humans anyway).

Figure 7.4

If you need to trim either end of the file, adjust its volume or even add an equaliser preset (not really recommended) basic mastering facilities can be found in the Song Information dialogue (select the file and use File > Get Info) on the Options page.

Last but not least, select the song and from the iTunes Advanced menu choose Convert Selection to MP3. You're done. The MP3 will show up in the same folder as the AIFF file.

Burn it

Before burning your songs to a CD decide which kind of disc will be most suitable for your listeners. iTunes gives you three choices: CD (plays in consumer CD players and your Mac's optical drive), MP3 (plays in some consumer CD players and your Mac's optical drive) and Data (can be used with your Mac's optical drive but will not play in a consumer CD player). When you've decided:

1 Open the iTunes preferences and click on the Burn icon.
2 Select the burner of your choice from the pop-up menu.
3 Choose a speed for burning (unless you experience problems burning, leave this as Maximum Possible).
4 Choose a Disc format.

If you choose to burn an audio CD you can specify the gap length between your tracks, in seconds. Checking the Use Sound Check box will normalise the tracks. In other words the quieter tracks will be raised in volume, to match the levels of the louder tracks. If you've mastered your tracks carefully, you'll not need this function.

iTunes will now burn the playlist that you created when you exported your songs from GarageBand. If you haven't already done so, create a new playlist (Command-N) and drag your songs over. iTunes will name your CD after the playlist title, so if that's not what you want, change it.

To burn a CD:

1 Select the playlist.
2 Click on the Burn Disc icon (iTunes tells you to insert a disc).
3 Pop a blank disc into your Mac's optical drive (iTunes checks the disc and if it's OK, tells you to click Burn).
4 Click on the Burn Disc icon again (iTunes burns your CD).

Internet distribution and promotion

OK, you've written some great songs and converted them to MP3 format – but where do you go from here? How do you get your songs heard.

A great way to obtain feedback from potential fans and other musicians is to submit your song to GarageBand.com (www.garageband.com). Firstly, you join their community and review and rate 30 songs submitted by other artists. The songs you review are chosen at random, by GarageBand.com, so no favouritism is involved.

Once you've completed your reviews you can submit your own song which will be subjected to the same random review procedure, by other GarageBand.com members. If you consistently receive high rankings you'll move up the GarageBand.com charts.

GarageBand.com's charts are watched closely by the music industry and several top-ranking artists have been signed by major labels. Many more have received publishing or licensing deals. You may prefer to upload your music to a smaller site.

Info

Keeping your songs in an iTunes playlist makes it easy to transfer them over to an iPod and integrate them with other iLife applications. They can be used to accompany slide shows and movies in iPhoto and iMovie respectively. And if you have a DVD drive and a powerful Mac you can use them in iDVD too.

But at GarageBand.com the opportunity to earn unbiased feedback and recognition based on the merits of the music itself is a big attraction for many musicians.

In addition to the charts GarageBand.com also offers a range of free and paid services to musicians, such as gig promotion and advice from industry experts.

Figure 7.5
Sign up with
GarageBand.com and you
can host a web page, sell
your songs, promote gigs
and receive reviews

Appendix
Music Maker's spec sheets

The eMac

Processor: 1.25GHz PowerPC G4.
Memory: 256MB of RAM – supports up to 1GB.
Hard disk: Ultra ATA/100 40GB (Combo Drive) and 80GB (SuperDrive).
Optical drive: Combo (DVD-ROM/CD-RW), SuperDrive (DVD-R/CD-RW).
Display: 17 inch (16 inch viewable) flat CRT.
Peripheral connections: Two FireWire, three USB 2.0 (on computer), two USB 1.1
(on keyboard).
Audio: One line in jack , one headphone jack, integrated stereo system.

Music related software
GarageBand
iTunes
Sound Studio

The iMac

Processor: Power PC G5, 1.6GHz and 1.8GHz options.
Memory: 256MB – supports up to 2GB.
Hard disk: 80GB or 160GB Serial ATA -7200 rpm.
Optical drive: Combo and SuperDrive options.
Display: 17 and 20 inch options.
Peripheral connections: Two FireWire, three USB 2.0 (on computer), two USB 1.1
(on keyboard).
Audio: One line in jack, headphone/optical digital audio output, Internal 12-watt
digital amplifier, built-in stereo speakers.

Music related software
GarageBand
iTunes

The iBook

Processor: 1.2GHz or 1.33GHz PowerPC G4.
Memory: 256MB supports up to 1.25GB (1 available slot).
Hard disk: 30GB or 60GB ATA/100 – 4200rpm.
Optical drive: Combo and SuperDrive options.
Display: 17 and 14 inch models.
Peripheral connections: One FireWire, two USB 2.0.
Audio: Headphone jack, built-in stereo speakers.

Music related software
GarageBand
iTunes

The PowerBook

Processor: 1.5GHz or 1.67GHz PowerPC G4.
Memory: 512MB expandable to 2GB (1.25GB on 12 inch model).
Hard disk: 60GB, 80GB or 100GB (17-inch) Ultra ATA/100. 5400-rpm.
Optical drive: Combo and SuperDrive options.
Display: 12, 15 and 17 inch models.
Peripheral connections: Two FireWire (only one on 12 inch model), two USB 2.0, one PC Card/CardBus slot (15 and 17-inch models)
Audio: One stereo line in, one headphone out, built-in stereo speakers (3rd, midrange-enhancing speaker on 12 and 15 inch models), internal omnidirectional microphone. Digital in/out on 17-inch models.

Music related software
GarageBand
iTunes

The Power Mac

Processor: 1.8Ghz, dual 1.8GHz, 2GHz or dual 2.5GHz 64-bit PowerPC G5.
Memory: 1.8GHz and dual 1.8GHz systems – 256MB, supports up to 4GB. Dual 2GHz and 2.5GHz systems – 512 GB, supports up to 8GB.
Hard disk: 1.8GHz and dual 1.8GHz systems – 80GB Serial ATA.
Dual 2GHz and 2.5GHz systems – 160GB Serial ATA.
Optical drive: SuperDrive (DVD-R/CD-RW).
Display: Separate monitor required.
PCI slots: 1.8GHz and dual 1.8GHz systems – Three open full-length 33MHz 64-bit slots.
Dual 2GHz and 2.5GHz systems – Three open full-length PCI-X slots: one 133MHz, 64-bit slot and two 100MHz, 64-bit slots.
Expansion: One FireWire 800 port, two FireWire 400 ports (one on fron); three USB 2.0 ports (one on front), two USB 1.1 ports (on keyboard).
Audio: Optical digital audio input, optical didital audio output, analogue audio input, analogue audio output, front headphone minijack and speaker.

Music related software
GarageBand
iTunes
Quicktime

The Mac mini

Processor: 1.25GHz or 1.42GHz PowerPC G4.
Memory: 256MB, supports up to 1GB.
Hard disk: 40GB (1.25GHz) and 80GB (1.42GHz).
Optical drive: Combo Drive (DVD-R/CD-RW) or SuperDrive (DVD±RW/CD-RW.
Display: None.
Peripheral connections: One FireWire 400 port; two USB 2.0 ports.
Audio: Headphone/audio line out. Built-in speaker.

Music related software
GarageBand
iTunes

Index